FlashKids SUMMER

1st Grade

Jumpstart first grade with fun skill-building activities!

FlashKids

New York

Flash Kids
New York

An Imprint of Sterling Publishing Co., Inc.

ISBN 978-1-4114-8064-3

Distributed in Canada by Sterling Publishing Co., Inc.
c/o Canadian Manda Group, 664 Annette Street
Toronto, Ontario, M6S 2C8, Canada
Distributed in the United Kingdom by GMC Distribution Services
Castle Place, 166 High Street, Lewes, East Sussex, BN7 1XU, England
Distributed in Australia by NewSouth Books
University of New South Wales, Sydney, NSW 2052, Australia

For information about custom editions, special sales, and premium and corporate purchases, please contact Sterling Special Sales at specialsales@sterlingpublishing.com.

Manufactured in Malaysia
Lot #:
2 4 6 8 10 9 7 5 3 1
11/21

sterlingpublishing.com

Cover illustration: Justin Poulter

Front cover image: somethingway/iStock/Getty Images Plus
Back cover image: Samuel Borges Photography/Shutterstock.com
All interior images by Depositphotos, iStockphoto, Shutterstock, Thinkstock, and Wikimedia Foundation with the following exception:
© Dorling Kindersley/Getty Images (map).

Dear Caregiver,

As a caregiver, you want your child to have time to relax and have fun during the summer, but you don't want your child's math and reading skills to get rusty. How do you make time for summer fun while ensuring that your child will be ready for the next school year?

The *Flash Kids Summer* workbook provides short, fun activities to help children keep their skills fresh all summer long. This book not only reviews what students learned during kindergarten, it also introduces what they'll be learning in first grade. Best of all, the games, puzzles, and stories help students retain their knowledge as well as build new skills. By the time your child finishes the book, they will be ready for a smooth transition into the next school year.

As your child completes the activities in this book, shower them with encouragement and praise. You can feel good knowing that you are taking an active and important role in your child's education. Helping your child complete the activities in this book is providing an excellent example—that you value learning every day! Have a wonderful summer, and most of all have fun learning together!

Bubbly B

Follow the directions below.

bed

we**b**

Practice writing the letters **Bb**.

Write **Bb** if the picture **begins** with the **b** sound.

_____   _____   _____   _____

Write **Bb** if the picture **ends** with the **b** sound.

_____   _____   _____   _____

Two Tulips

Connect the numbers **1** through **10** to trace the tulips.

C Is For...

Follow the directions below.

<u>c</u>at

Practice writing the letters **Cc**.

Circle the pictures that begin with the **c** sound.

Count and Add

Look at the objects. Write the math sentence.
Then add the numbers. The first one is done for you.

1.  +
   _2_ + _1_ = _3_

2.  +
   _____ + _____ = _____

3. +
   _____ + _____ = _____

4. +
   _____ + _____ = _____

5. +
   _____ + _____ = _____

6. +
   _____ + _____ = _____

7. +
   _____ + _____ = _____

8. +
   _____ + _____ = _____

Which Is Less?

Count the objects in each group. Write the number of objects in each group.
Circle the group with the smaller number.

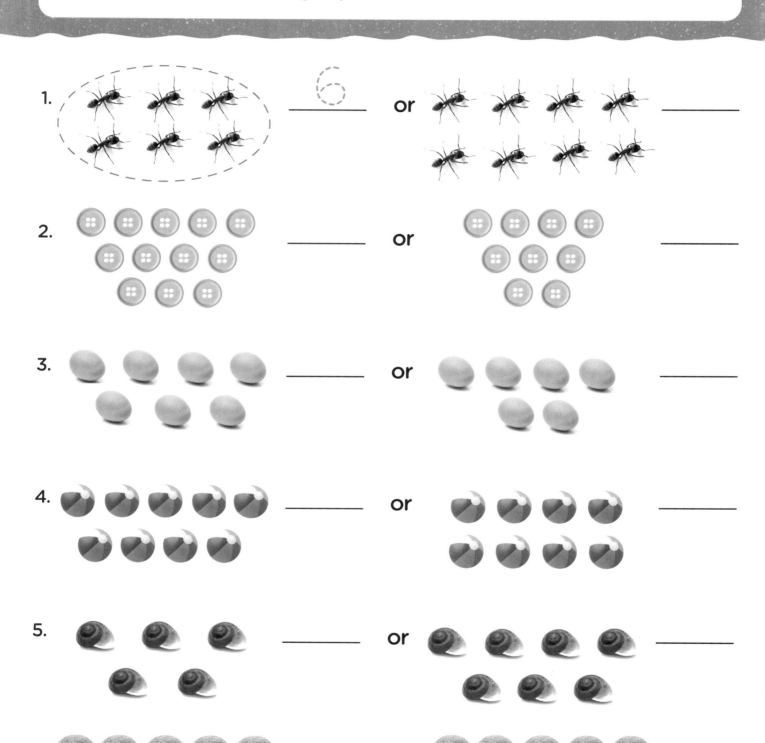

1. _____ 6 or _____

2. _____ or _____

3. _____ or _____

4. _____ or _____

5. _____ or _____

6. _____ or _____

Numbers Fun

Color the number of boxes for each row. The first one is done for you.

2					
4					
1					
3					
5					

Find the numbers **1, 2, 3, 4,** and **5** and circle them.

4	I	E	S	5
O	L	1	R	3
P	C	X	2	Q

Doghouse D

Follow the directions below.

dog

sa**d**

Practice writing the letters **Dd**.

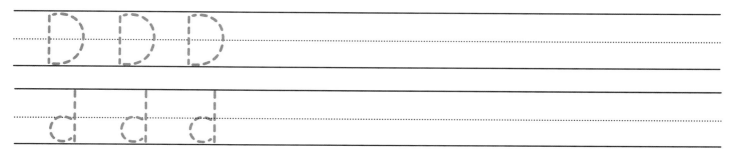

Draw a line from each picture to the correct doghouse.

Beginning **D**

Ending **D**

Colorful Crayons

Trace the color word. Then draw a line to the matching crayon.

1. red

2. yellow

3. orange

4. black

5. purple

6. blue

7. brown

8. green

Sound Search

Look at each picture. Say the name aloud. What is the first sound in the word? Circle the letter for that sound.

1. n (m) g

2. l b c

3. d b r

4. w f y

5. t r s

6. h j s

7. b m l

8. p g n

9. d g p

10. t f k

11. r s q

12. b n d

Balloon Bunches

Draw the number of balloons that equals the number.

Alphaball

Fill in the uppercase or lowercase letters in **ABC** order.

ABC
DEF
GHI
JKL
MNO
PQR
STU
VWX
YZ

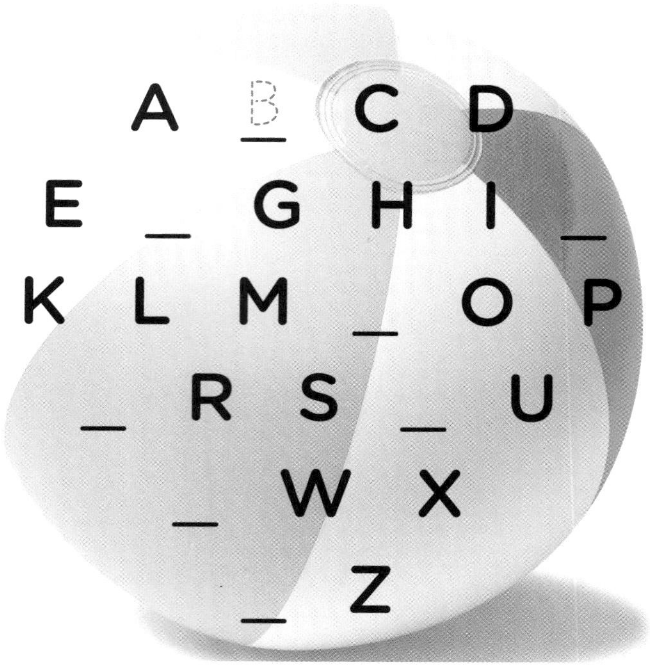

A _ C D
E _ G H I _
K L M _ O P
_ R S _ U
_ W X
_ Z

abc
def
ghi
jkl
mno
pqr
stu
vwx
yz

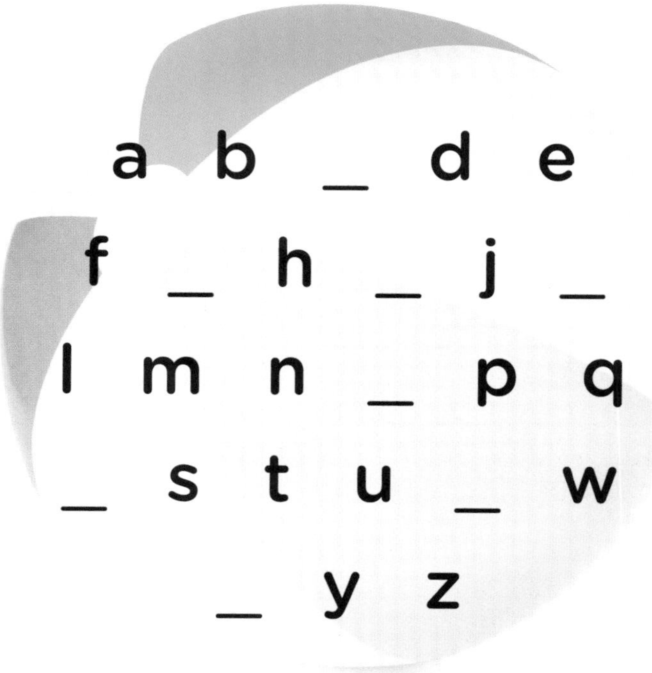

a b _ d e
f _ h _ j _
l m n _ p q
_ s t u _ w
_ y z

All About Me!

Ask an adult to help you write about yourself on the lines below.
Then tape a photo or draw a picture of yourself in the box.

My name is _____.

I am _____ years old.

I was born on _____.

I have _____ hair.

I have _____ eyes.

My favorite food is _____.

My favorite color is _____.

My favorite book is _____.

My favorite movie is _____.

I live in _____.

My favorite things to do are _____

_____

_____.

When I grow up, I want to be a _____

_____

_____.

Me

Get in Shape!

Connect the matching shapes. Write the letter your line crosses below.

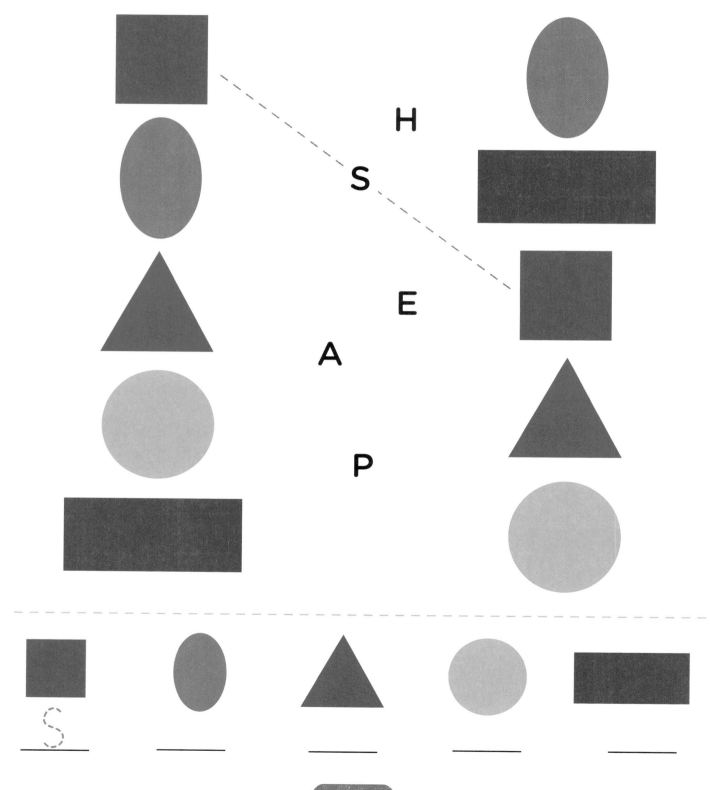

H

S

E

A

P

S

All Short A

Follow the directions below.

d<u>a</u>d

Practice writing the letters **Aa**.

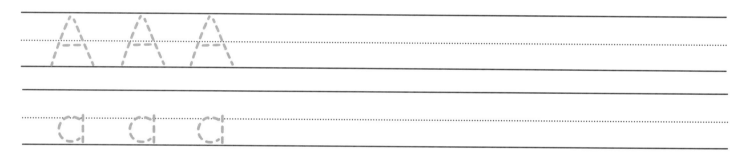

Write the vowel **a** to complete each word.
Draw a line from the word to the matching picture.

_nt

c_p

b_g

r_t

What Does Not Belong?

Circle the object in each row that does not belong.

1.

2.

3.

4.

5.

6.

Telling Time

Look at each clock. Write the time shown.

1.

_____ : _____

2.

_____ : _____

3.

_____ : _____

4.

_____ : _____

5.

_____ : _____

6.

_____ : _____

Train of Ten

Follow the directions below.

Trace the numbers **1 to 10**.

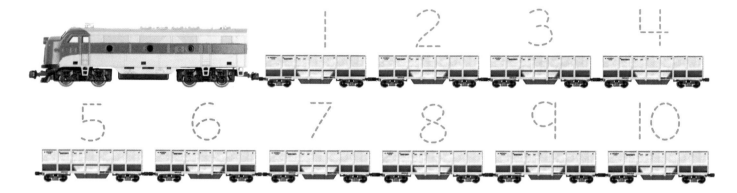

Write the missing numbers.

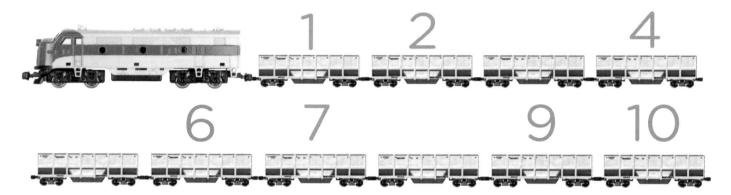

Write the numbers **1 to 10**.

Fish Fun

Follow the directions below.

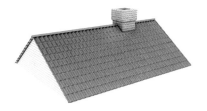

fish

roo**f**

Practice writing the letters **Ff**.

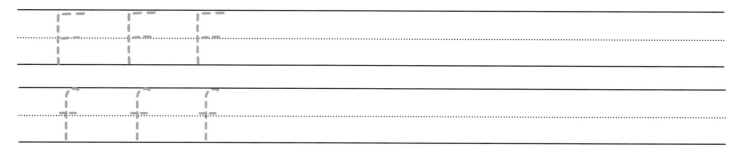

Write **Ff** if the picture **begins** with the **f** sound.

_____

_____

_____

Write **Ff** if the picture **ends** with the **f** sound.

_____

_____

_____

Animal Alphabet

Write the names of these animals in alphabetical order.

fox

snake

ape

cat

deer

whale

mouse

lion

bear

owl

pig

hippo

1. ape _____

2. _____

3. _____

4. _____

5. _____

6. _____

7. _____

8. _____

9. _____

10. _____

11. _____

12. _____

Goldfish Game

Follow the directions below.

gum

bu**g**

Practice writing the letters **Gg**.

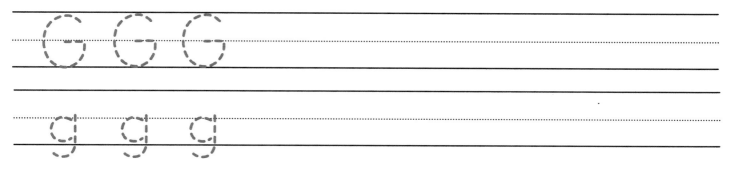

Draw a line from each picture to the correct fish bowl.

Beginning **G**

Ending **G**

At the End

Say the name of each object aloud. What sound do you hear at the end?
Trace the letters for each word. Then write the ending letter.

1.

ja __r__

2.

pai ___

3.

do ___

4.

sto ___

5.

fa ___

6.

ba ___

7.

be ___

8.

loc ___

A Pretty Plant

Label each part of the plant. Use words from the box.

stem   flower   leaf   roots

1. flower

2. _____

3. _____

4. _____

Super Sizes

Follow the directions below.

Circle the picture that is **bigger** than the first one in the row.

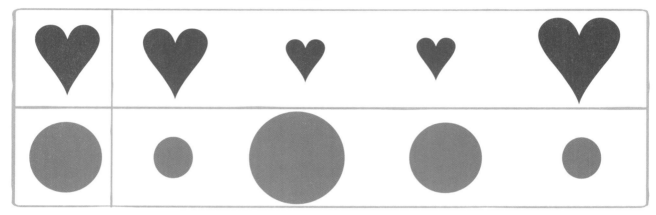

Circle the picture that is **smaller** than the first one in the row.

Circle the picture that is the **same size** as the first one in the row.

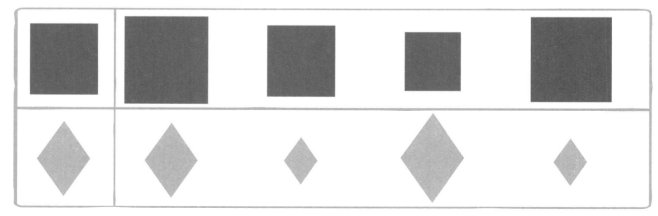

How He Hopped

Follow the directions below.

hug

Practice writing the letters **Hh**.

H H H

h h h

How did the frog hop across the pond to the log?
Circle the pictures that begin with the **h** sound.

Caring and Sharing

It's important to be nice to others. Circle the pictures that show children caring for and sharing with each other.

Shapes, Shapes, Shapes!

Look at each picture below. What shape do you see?
Write the shape word under each picture.

circle

square

triangle

1.

circle

_____

2.

_____

3.

_____

4.

_____

5.

_____

6.

_____

7.

_____

8.

_____

9.

_____

Box of Balloons

Follow the directions below.

Circle the group with **more** balloons.

Circle the group with **fewer** balloons.

Lost Letters

Draw a line to match the letter pairs **Aa** through **Zz**.

A   M   S   e   E

T   a   W   m   C

   X   j   p   c   P   Y

G   x   D
   J   w   s   y   k   z

t   b   l

F   N   B   d   O   K

        g   o
   q   v   L   R   Z
                                   I
              n   i   H   h

Q   f   V   u   r   U

Finish the Pattern

Look at the shapes and colors in each row. Finish each pattern.

1.  _____ _____

2. _____ _____ _____

3. _____ _____ _____

4. _____ _____ _____

5.  _____ _____ _____ _____

6. _____ _____ _____ _____

Awesome Addition

Add the numbers.

1. $4 + 1 = 5$

2. $2 + 2 =$

3. $0 + 5 =$

4. $3 + 4 =$

5. $3 + 2 =$

6. $1 + 1 =$

7. $2 + 0 =$

8. $3 + 3 =$

9. $2 + 4 =$

10. $6 + 0 =$

11. $3 + 5 =$

12. $4 + 4 =$

13. $6 + 1 =$

14. $5 + 5 =$

15. $0 + 1 =$

16. $8 + 1 =$

Coin Connection

Connect the matching coins. Write how much each is worth below.

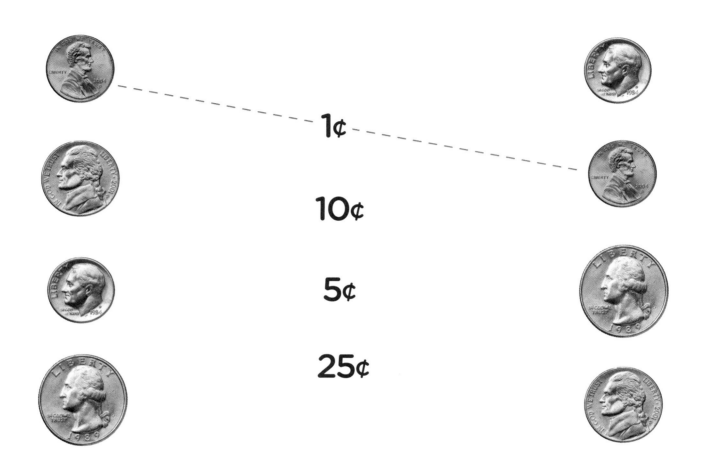

1¢

10¢

5¢

25¢

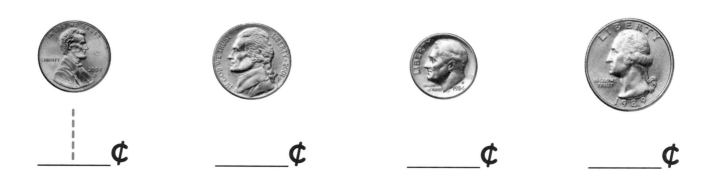

_____ ¢   _____ ¢   _____ ¢   _____ ¢

Short E Everywhere

Follow the directions below.

p<u>e</u>n

Practice writing the letters **Ee**.

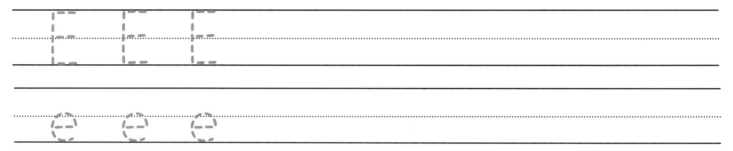

Write the vowel **e** to complete each word.
Draw a line from the word to the matching picture.

h _ n

b _ ll

_ gg

n _ t

Hooray for Long A!

The **a** sound you hear in the word **cake** is the **long a** sound.
Say the name of each object. Circle the objects that have the **long a** sound.

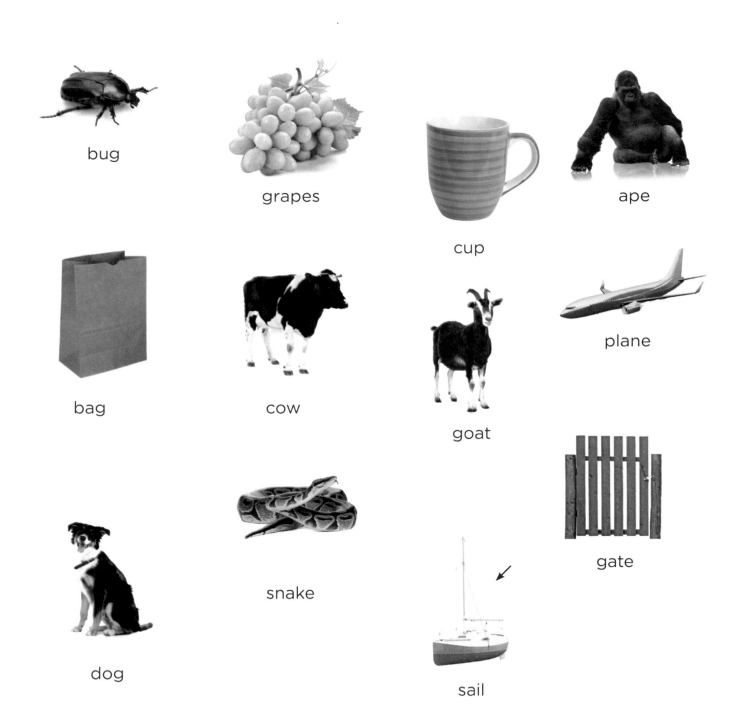

bug

grapes

cup

ape

bag

cow

goat

plane

dog

snake

sail

gate

See the Long E!

The **e** sound you hear in the word **feet** is the **long e** sound.
Say the name of each object. Circle the objects that have the **long e** sound.

kite

hen

seal

bee

clock

doll

bed

sheep

deer

tree

leaf

book

Silly Shapes

Draw the next shape in the pattern.

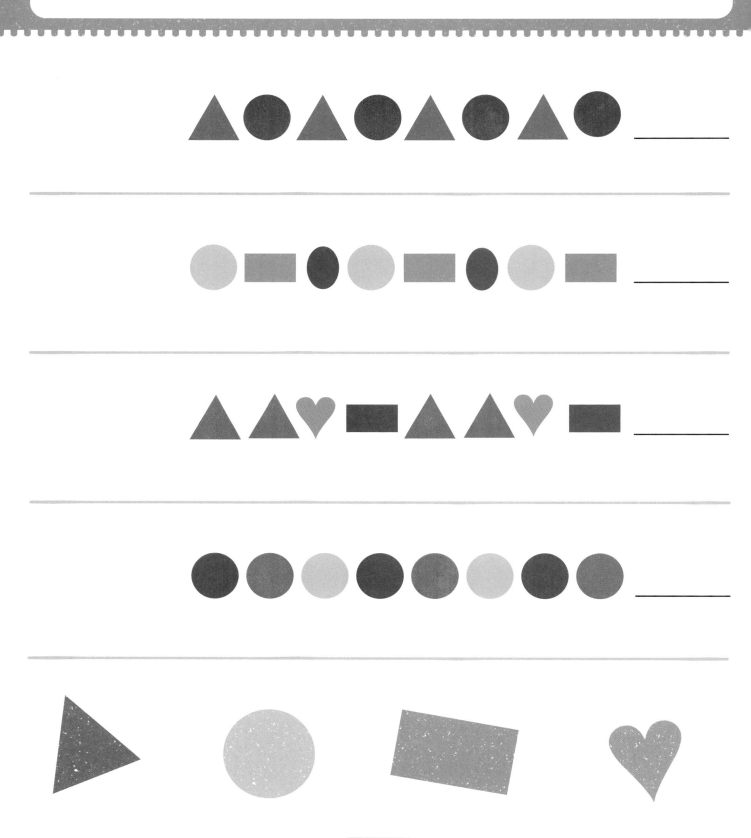

Jelly Bean Journey

Follow the directions below.

jet

Practice writing the letters **Jj**.

How did Jan get across the pond to the jelly beans?
Circle the pictures that begin with the **j** sound.

Picture Puzzle

Draw a line to match each word to its picture.

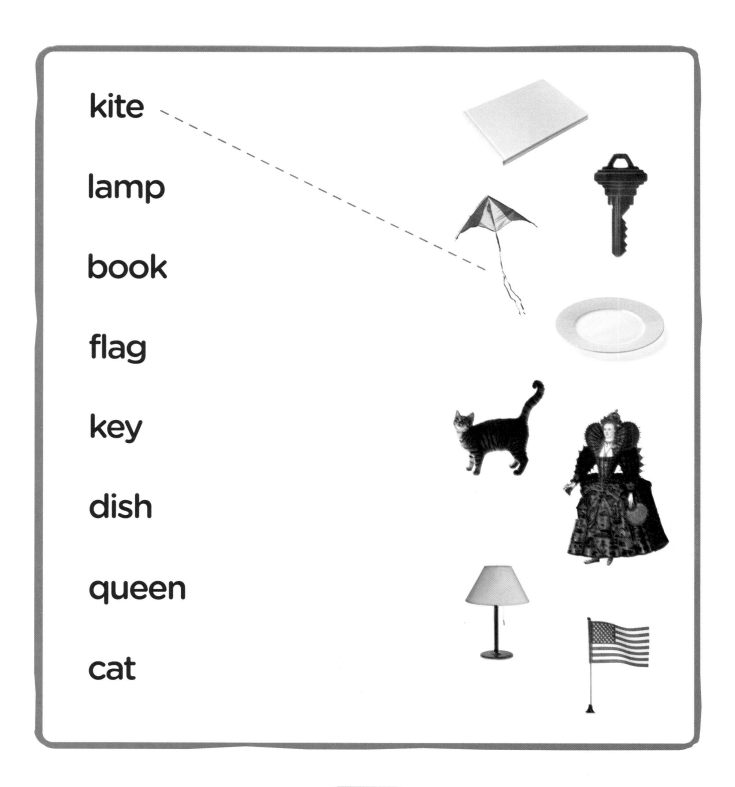

kite

lamp

book

flag

key

dish

queen

cat

Places on Earth

Read the names in the box. Then write each name under its matching picture.

rain forest   desert   ocean   forest

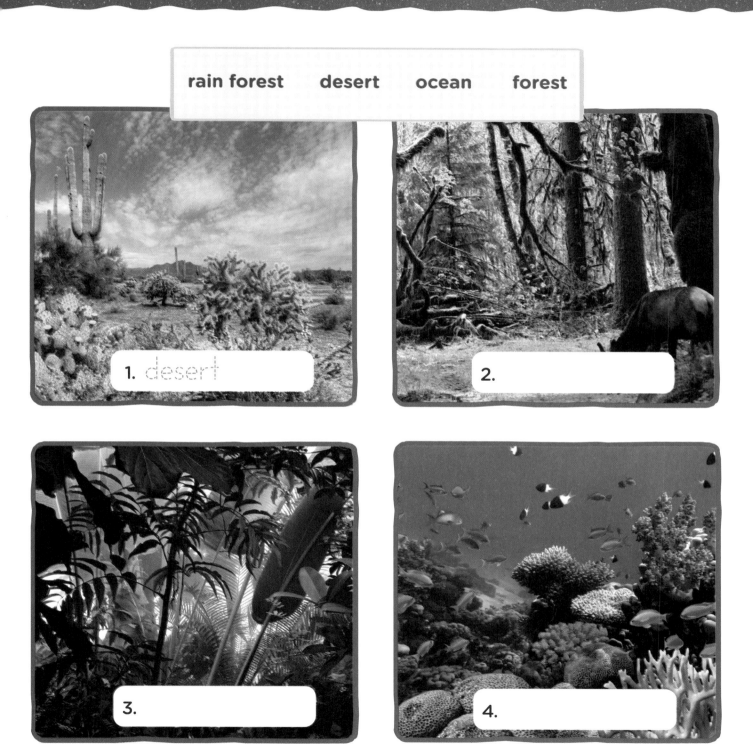

1. desert

2.

3.

4.

Kite Tails

Follow the directions below.

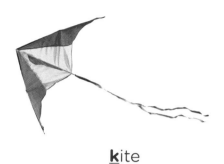

kite

lea**k**

Practice writing the letters **Kk**.

Write **Kk** if the picture **begins** with the **k** sound.

Beginning **K**

_____   _____   _____

Write **Kk** if the picture **ends** with the **k** sound.

Ending **K**

_____   _____   _____

I Know My Country

Follow the directions below.

Trace the words for each American symbol.

This is the American flag .

It has 50 stars and 13 stripes.

This is a bald eagle.

It is the American national bird.

This is the Statue of Liberty.

It is a symbol of freedom.

Write one thing you know about one of these American symbols.

_____

_____

_____

_____

_____

Change Challenge

Circle the coins to match the amount shown.

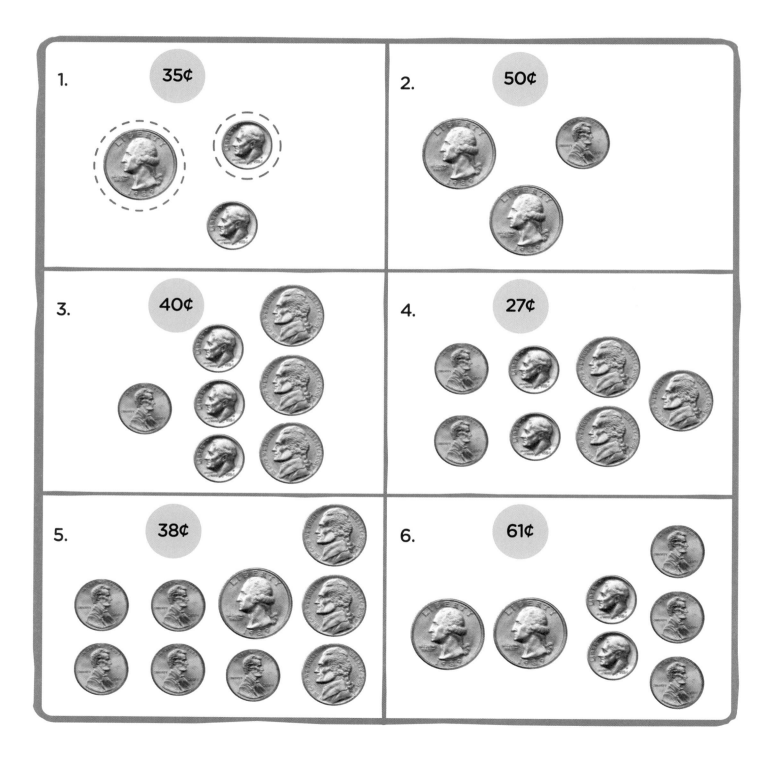

1. 35¢

2. 50¢

3. 40¢

4. 27¢

5. 38¢

6. 61¢

Pattern Power

Complete the patterns.

Leafy L

Follow the directions below.

leg   seal

Practice writing the letters **Ll**.

Draw a line from each picture to the correct tree.

Beginning **L**   Ending **L**

Weighing In

Follow the directions below.

Circle the heavier object in each box.

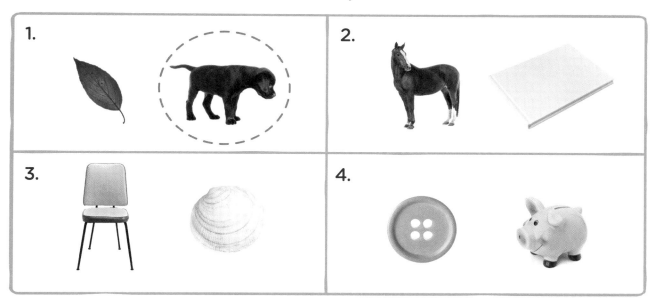

Circle the lighter object in each box.

Measuring Mail

Use a ruler to measure each piece of mail.

1. *2 inches* _____

2. _____

3. _____

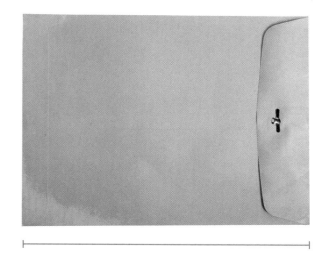

4. _____

5. _____

Balloon Buddies

Draw a line to connect the matching balloon pairs.

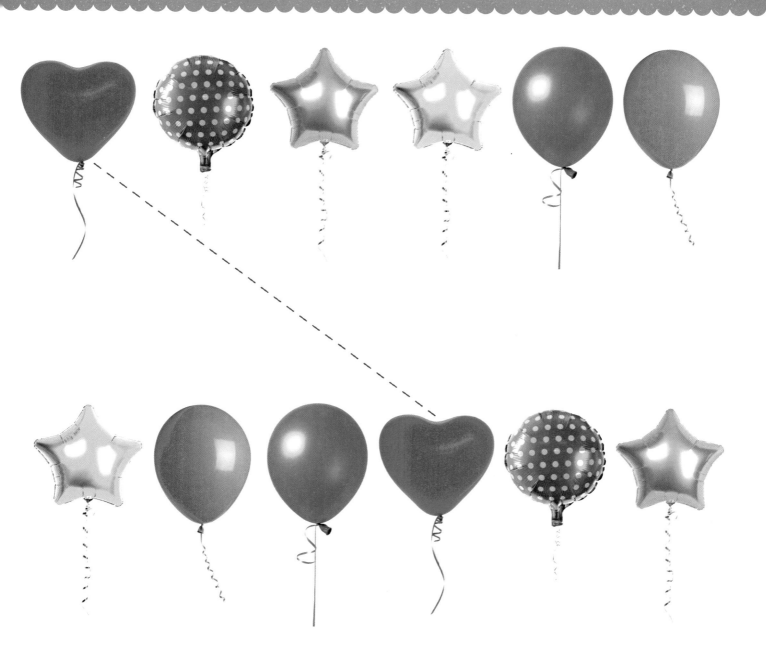

Letter Mix-up

Below are the mixed-up letters of a word. How many little words can you make from the letters? Can you find the BIG word?

a   n   t   i   r

Words with 2 letters:

_____

_____

_____

_____

Words with 3 letters:

_____

_____

_____

_____

_____

_____

Word with 4 letters:

_____

The BIG word:

_____

Draw a picture of the BIG word below. Here's a hint: It is a fun way to travel.

Day at the Beach

Look at the summer words in the word box. Find and circle the words in the word search. They can go across or down.

sun	shell	fish	sand
waves	sea	pail	crab

```
F   I   S   H   R   W
J   A   U   S   E   A
I   S   N   H   D   V
N   C   O   E   B   E
A   R   W   L   O   S
P   A   I   L   R   E
O   B   S   A   N   D
```

Count and Match

Match each picture with the correct number.

 = 10

11

12

13

14

15

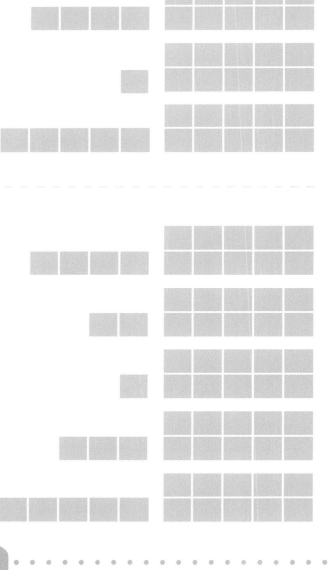

11

12

13

14

15

Short I Wins!

Follow the directions below.

p_i_n

Practice writing the letters **Ii**.

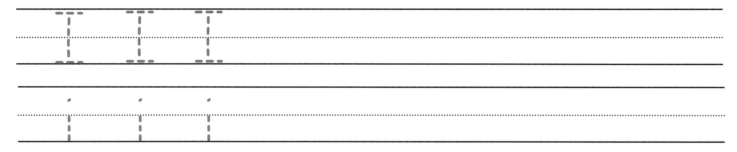

Write the vowel **i** to complete each word.
Draw a line from the word to the matching picture.

h _ ll

d _ g

p _ g

k _ d

Hi, Long I!

The **i** sound you hear in the word **smile** is the **long i** sound.
Say the name of each object. Circle the objects that have the **long i** sound.

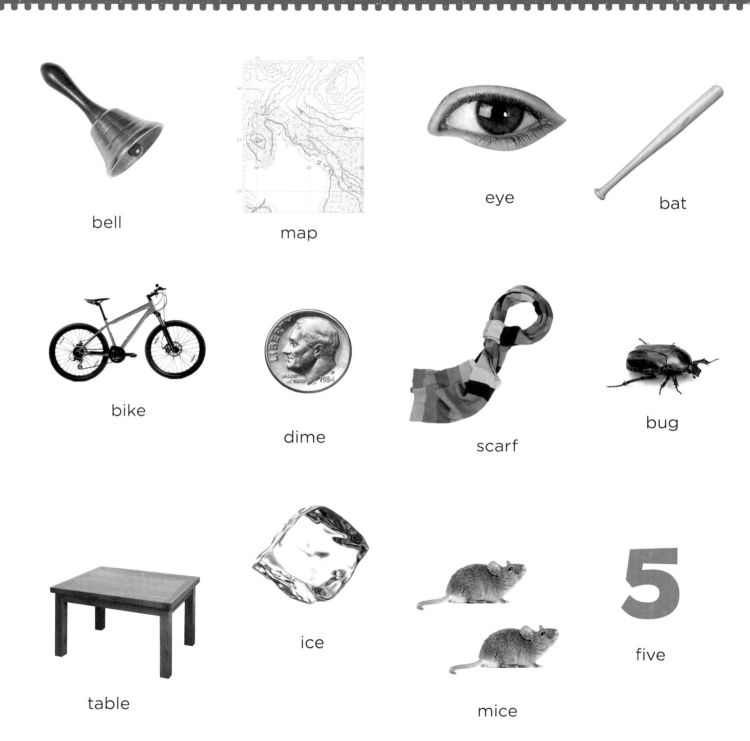

bell

map

eye

bat

bike

dime

scarf

bug

table

ice

mice

five

Mothers and Babies

Follow the directions below.

Draw a line to match each mother animal to her baby.

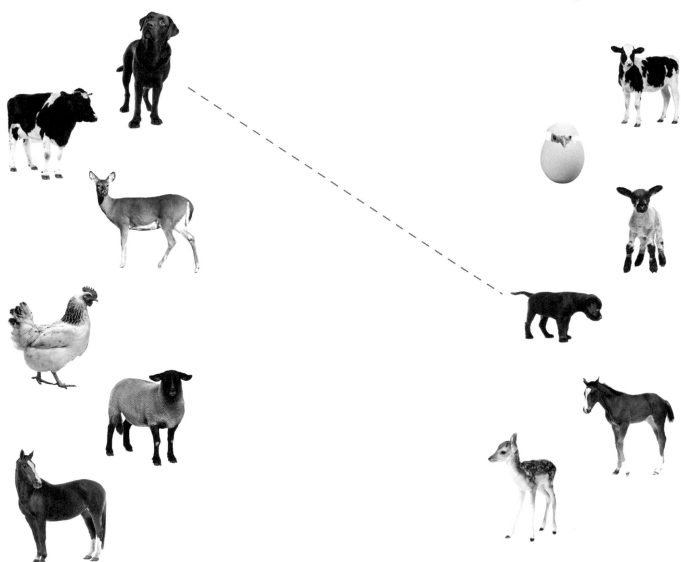

Write the baby animal names.

1. Baby dog: p u ___ ___ ___

2. Baby chicken: c h ___ ___ ___

3. Baby cow: c a ___ ___

4. Baby sheep: l a ___ ___

5. Baby deer: f a ___ ___

6. Baby horse: f o ___ ___

Train Car Totals

Follow the directions below.

Count the cars, then write the number on the line.

1.

_____

2.

_____

Count the cars, then add one more car to the end. Write the total on the line.

3.

_____

4.

_____

5.

_____

Mailbox Match

Follow the directions below.

map

ha**m**

Practice writing the letters **Mm**.

Draw a line from each picture to the correct mailbox.

Beginning **M**

Ending **M**

In a Minute

Look at each picture. Does each activity take
more or less than one minute? Circle **more** or **less**.

1. Eating lunch

(more)   less

2. Writing your name

more   less

3. Riding a bike to school

more   less

4. Reading a book

more   less

5. Blowing out candles

more   less

6. Kicking a ball

more   less

Take Your Time

Follow the directions below.

Look at the pictures in each box. Circle the thing that takes **more** time.

About how long would it take? Circle the answer.

30 seconds   30 minutes

2 minutes   2 seconds

4 minutes   4 hours

Get in with N!

Follow the directions below.

__n__ap   pe__n__

Practice writing the letters **Nn**.

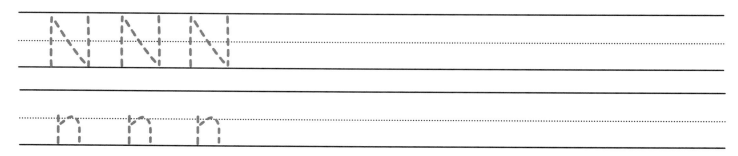

Write **Nn** if the picture begins with the **n** sound.

Beginning **N**

_____   _____   _____

Write **Nn** if the picture ends with the **n** sound.

    Ending **N**

_____   _____   _____

Sunday Is a Fun Day

Follow the directions below.

Trace the name of each day of the week.

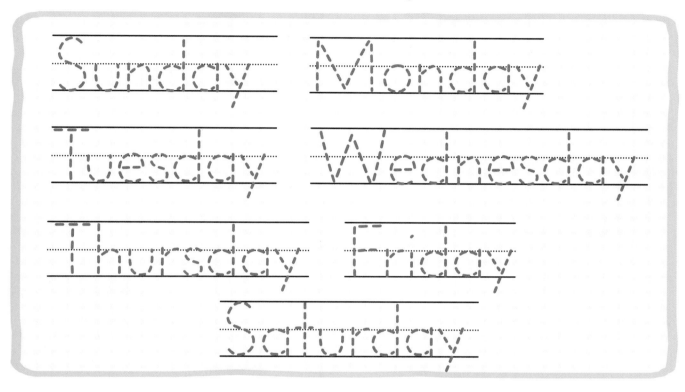

What is your favorite day of the week? Write the name of the day.
Then draw a picture of something you like to do on that day.

_____

....

_____

Cat Tails

How long is each cat's tail? Count the units.

1. Sam's tail is ____5____ units long.

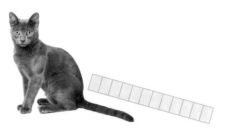

2. Scratchy's tail is _____ units long.

3. Puff's tail is _____ units long.

4. Teeny's tail is _____ units long.

5. Stubby's tail is _____ units long.

How Many Pennies?

Follow the directions below.

Add the pennies, then write the total.

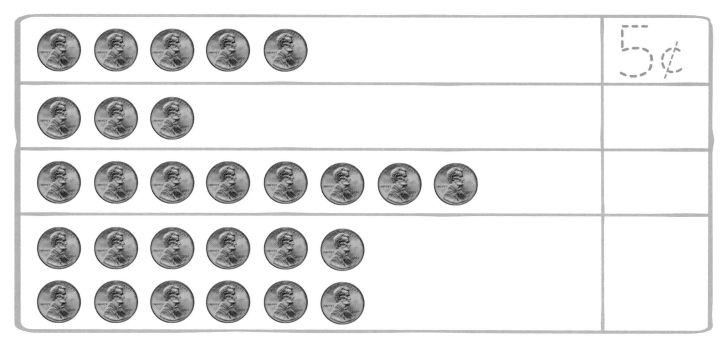

Circle pennies to equal the amount on the left.

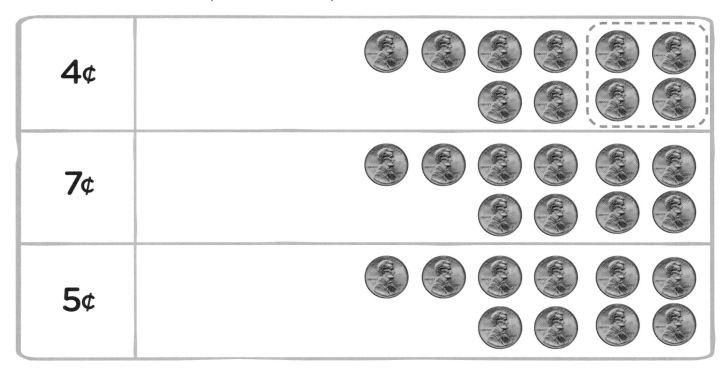

Pat's Path

Follow the directions below.

pot

ho**p**

Practice writing the letters **Pp**.

Help Pat get to his prize! Connect the pictures that **begin** with the **p** sound and follow the path. Then connect the pictures that **end** with the **p** sound and follow the path.

Ending **P**

Beginning **P**

Opposite Match

Draw a line matching the opposites below.

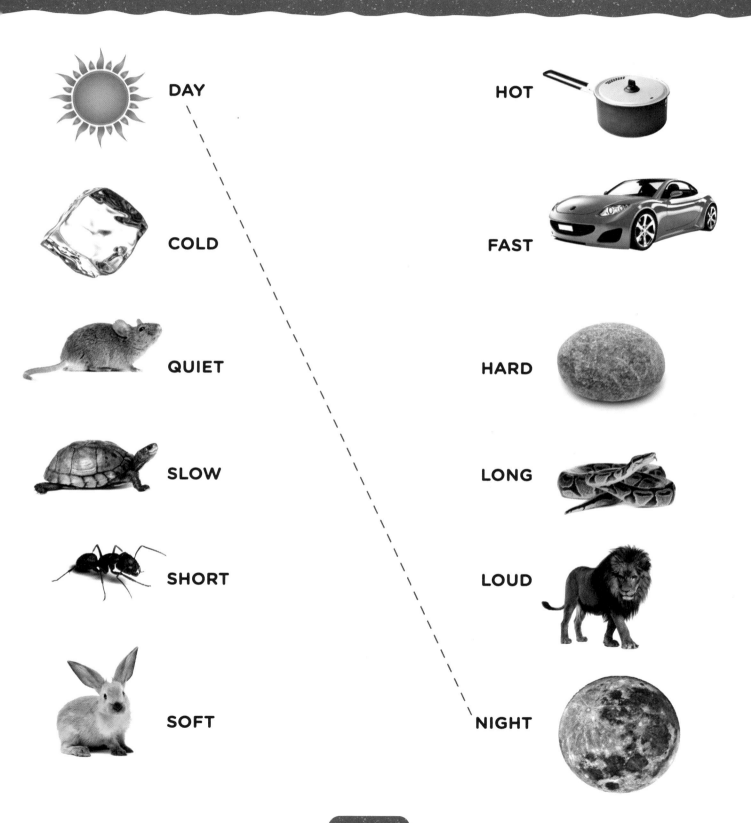

DAY

COLD

QUIET

SLOW

SHORT

SOFT

HOT

FAST

HARD

LONG

LOUD

NIGHT

Sound It Out

Look at each picture. Sound it out. Then write the beginning and ending letters for each word.

1. c o a t

2. __ e a __

3. __ o a __

4. __ e a __

5. __ o a __

6. __ e a __

7. __ o a __

8. __ e a __

Bye-bye, Balloon

Follow the directions below.

One balloon floated away from each group. Count the balloons and subtract.

5 – 1 = 4

1.

7 – 1 = 6

2.

9 – ___ = ___

3.

4 – 1 = ___

4.

___ – ___ = ___

If all the balloons float away, there are 0 left.

5.

2 – 2 = ___

6.

3 – 3 = ___

Hide and Seek

The word on the left is hiding in the sentences. Circle it each time you see it.

1. **you**

You go hide.
We will find you.

2. **not**

Do not come.
We are not ready!

3. **in**

What's in the box?
You are not in the box!

4. **we**

We are not in that box.
Look where we are.

5. **go**

Go look in the box.
Now we can go hide.

Copy the words.

you _____

not _____

in _____

we _____

go _____

Hello, Long O!

The **o** sound you hear in the word **rose** is the long **o** sound.
Say the name of each object. Circle the objects that have the **long o** sound.

soap

snake

sheep

rope

hoe

spoon

toe

bow

fox

car

bird

The Four Seasons

There are four seasons. They are called **winter**, **spring**, **summer**, and **fall**.
Look at each object. Which season does it remind you of?
Write **winter**, **spring**, **summer**, or **fall**.

1. winter _____

2. _____

3. _____

4. _____

5. _____

6. _____

7. _____

8. _____

9. _____

10. _____

Time Lines

Match each clock to the correct time.

four o'clock   **7:00**

ten o'clock   **3:00**

seven o'clock   **2:00**

two o'clock   **9:00**

three o'clock   **4:00**

nine o'clock   **10:00**

Short O Objects

Follow the directions below.

t<u>o</u>p

Practice writing the letters **Oo**.

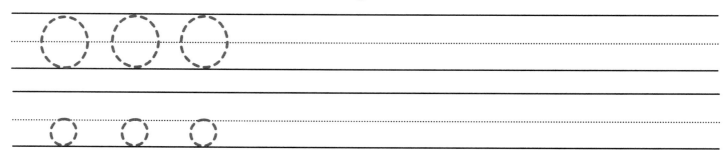

Write the vowel **o** to complete each word.
Draw a line from the word to the matching picture.

p _ t

s _ ck

B _ b

m _ p

Where Does It Come From?

Can you tell where things come from? Draw a line to match the three pictures that go together.

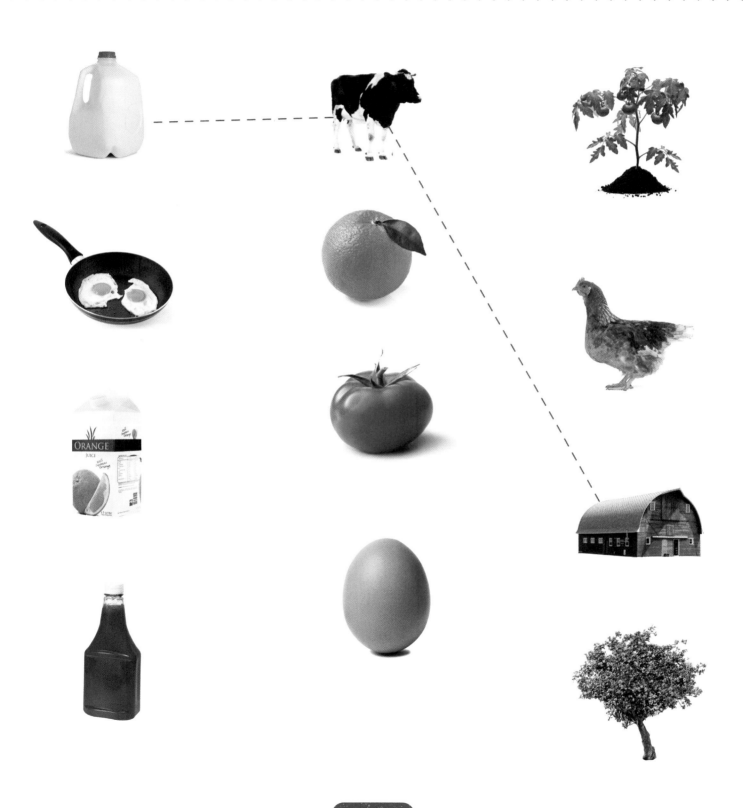

What Time Is It?

Draw the minute hand and the hour hand on each clock to show the time.

minute hand	⟶
hour hand	⟶

It's 9:30.

1.

7:30

2.

12:00

3.

9:00

4.

11:30

5.

6:00

6.

2:30

7.

5:30

8.

4:00

9.

10:00

Tagalong Train

More train cars want to tag along. Add the cars,
then write the total under the engine.

1.

4 + 2 =

_____

2.

3 + 2 =

_____

3.

5 + __ =

_____

4.

__ + 5 =

_____

5.

__ + __ =

_____

Queen's Quest

Follow the directions below.

quiz

Practice writing the letters **Qq**.

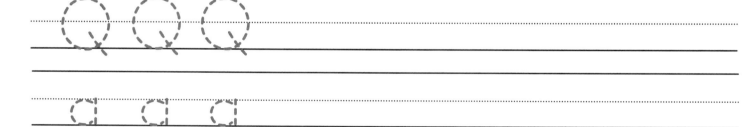

Circle the pictures that begin with the **q** sound.

Long U, Too!

The **u** sound you hear in the word **blue** is the **long u** sound. Say the name of each object. Circle the objects that have the **long u** sound.

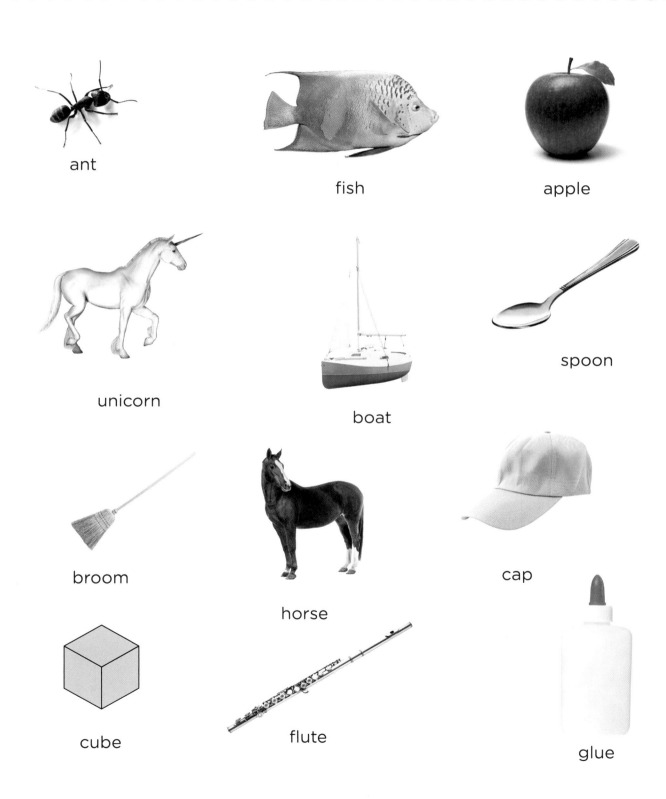

ant

fish

apple

unicorn

boat

spoon

broom

horse

cap

cube

flute

glue

Listen for Sounds

Say each word aloud. Then draw a line from each object on the left to an object on the right with the same short-vowel sound.

a as in **apple**   e as in **end**   i as in **inch**
o as in **ox**   u as in **up**

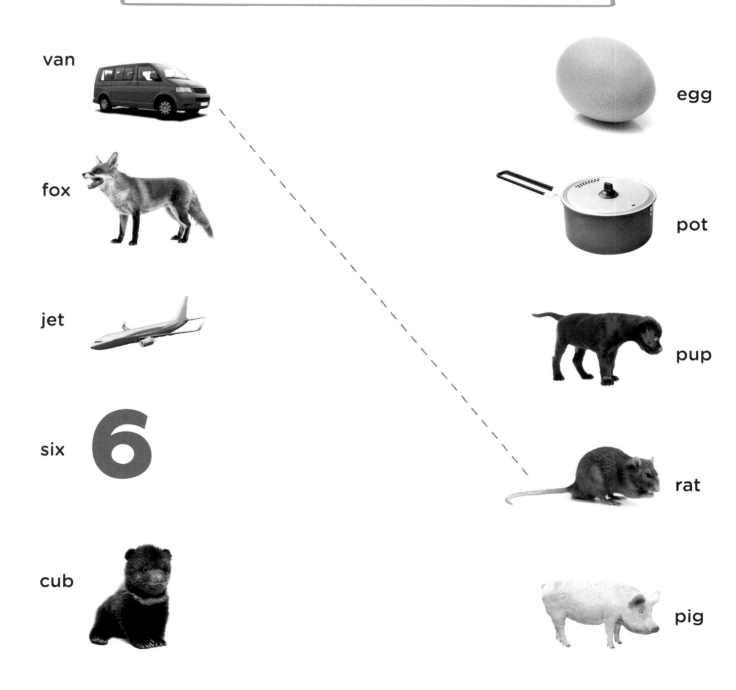

van

fox

jet

six

cub

egg

pot

pup

rat

pig

Race for First Place

Follow the directions below.

Kids were called to the track by the ABC order of their names.
Draw a line to show the order of the runners.

1st	Ted
2nd	Jen
3rd	Sam
4th	Kim
5th	Val

Now write the ordinal number next to each runner's name.

Ted: fourth

Jen: _____

Sam: _____

Val: _____

Kim: _____

Ready for R

Follow the directions below.

rug

ca**r**

Practice writing the letters **Rr**.

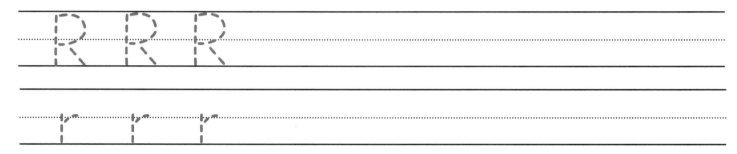

Write **Rr** if the picture **begins** with the **r** sound.

Beginning **R**

_____ _____ _____

Write **Rr** if the picture **ends** with the **r** sound.

Ending **R**

_____ _____ _____

Ready to Rhyme

Say the name for each picture. Then circle the words
in each row that rhyme with the picture word.

1. lid   (tune)   (noon)   bell

2. lake   rock   steak   box

3. boat   sand   bee   sea

4. sock   kite   jump   rock

5. snow   meet   ring   swing

6. well   rain   good   plane

My Five Senses

Write the name of the sense under the picture.

see   hear   smell   taste   feel

1. feel

2.

3.

4.

5.

6.

7.

8.

9.

Made in the Shade

Shade the squares, then cross out the number to be subtracted. Count how many are left and write the number.

5 - 3 = 2	X	X	X							
7 - 4 = ____										
6 - 2 = ____										
4 - 1 = ____										
3 - 0 = ____										
8 - 6 = ____										
2 - 1 = ____										
5 - 5 = ____										
10 - 4 = ____										

Soccer Sort

Follow the directions below.

<u>s</u>ub

bu<u>s</u>

Practice writing the letters **Ss**.

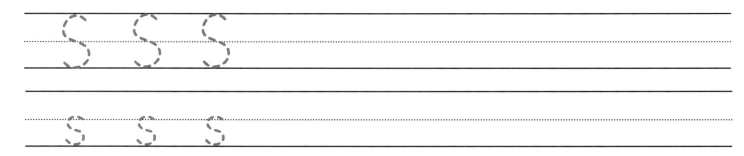

Draw a line from each object to the correct goal.

Beginning **S**

Ending **S**

My Community

Many people help us in our communities. Write the word that tells about each helper. Use the words in the box.

sick	pet	fires	read	teeth	safe

1. A doctor helps me when I am sick .

2. A teacher helps me to learn how to r_____ .

3. A firefighter puts out f_____ .

4. A vet helps me care for my p_____ .

5. A dentist helps me have healthy t_____ .

6. A police officer helps keep the community s_____ .

Draw a picture of your favorite community helper.

Cross It Out

Follow the directions to find the answers.

1.

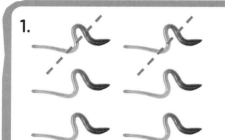

Cross out 2.

How many are left? __4__

2.

Cross out 3.

How many are left? _____

3.

Cross out 1.

How many are left? _____

4.

Cross out 3.

How many are left? _____

5.

Cross out 4.

How many are left? _____

6.

Cross out 2.

How many are left? _____

7.

Cross out 5.

How many are left? _____

8.

Cross out 4.

How many are left? _____

9.

Cross out 0.

How many are left? _____

Balloon Clues

Add or subtract. Use the balloons as picture clues.

1.

$3 + 4 = 7$

2.

$2 + 2 = \underline{}$

3.

$5 + \underline{} = \underline{}$

4.

$6 - 2 = 4$

5.

$8 - 3 = \underline{}$

6.

$10 - \underline{} = \underline{}$

Two Words Together

Two words join together to make a compound word.

sun + rise = sunrise

Join the two words together and write the compound word.

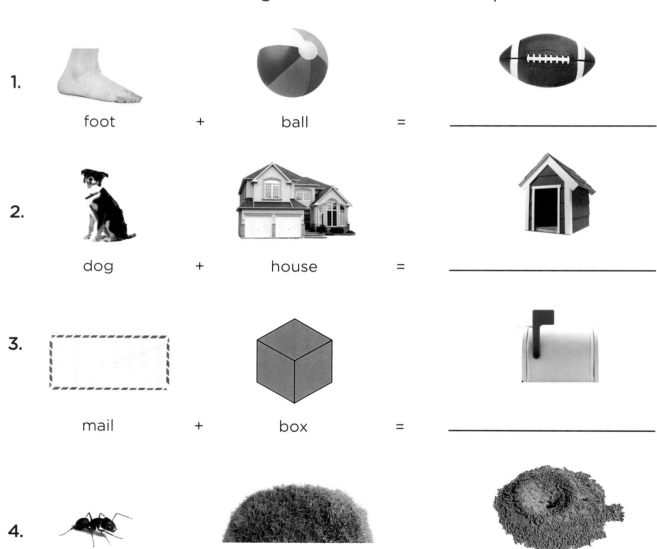

1. foot + ball = _____

2. dog + house = _____

3. mail + box = _____

4. ant + hill = _____

Listen Up!

Look at the objects in each group. Say the names of each aloud.
Then circle the short-vowel sound you hear in each group.

1. (a) e i o u

2. a e i o u

3. a e i o u

4. a e i o u

5. a e i o u

6 a e i o u

7. a e i o u

8. a e i o u

9. a e i o u

Halftime

Follow the directions below.

Draw a line to connect each picture with its other half.

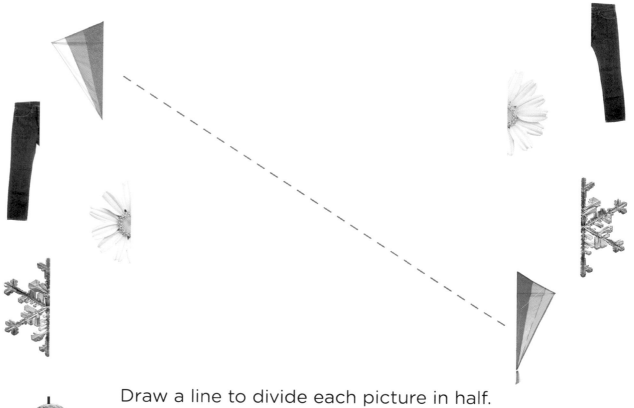

Draw a line to divide each picture in half.

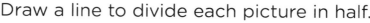

Now draw the other half.

You and Short U

Follow the directions below.

t**u**b

Practice writing the letters **Uu**.

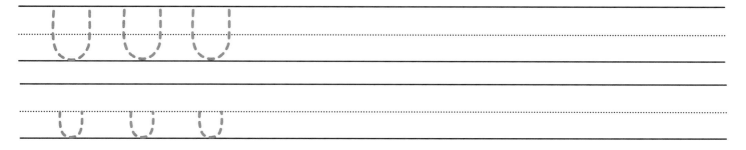

Write the vowel **u** to complete each word.
Draw a line from the word to the matching picture.

g _ m

b _ s

b _ g

s _ n

Kinds of Sentences

A **statement** tells something. It ends with a period (.).
A **question** asks something. It ends with a question mark (?).

Read each sentence aloud or have a parent read it to you.
Then tell if it is a **statement** or a **question**. Circle **S** or **Q**.

1. Mia loves to dance.   S   Q

2. The kite is in the tree.   S   Q

3. Did Josh eat the cookies?   S   Q

4. The ants are on the hill.   S   Q

5. Where are we going for lunch?   S   Q

6. Is the mouse under the bed?   S   Q

7. Jack played with his dog.   S   Q

8. I picked a daisy in the garden.   S   Q

9. Do you like ice cream?   S   Q

10. The long snake is red and black.   S   Q

What Will I Wear?

Circle the things you would wear or use in each kind of weather.

It is snowing.

It is sunny.

It is raining.

Tons of T

Follow the directions below.

<u>t</u>op

ba<u>t</u>

Practice writing the letters **Tt**.

Write **Tt** if the picture **begins** with the **t** sound.

Beginning **T**

10

_____ _____ _____

Write **Tt** if the picture **ends** with the **t** sound.

Ending **T**

_____ _____ _____

Staying Safe

Look at each picture. Some children are being safe. Some children are not being safe. Circle the pictures that show children being safe. Cross out the pictures that show children being unsafe.

Vans and Wagons

Follow the directions below.

<u>v</u>an

<u>w</u>agon

Practice writing the letters **Vv** and **Ww**.

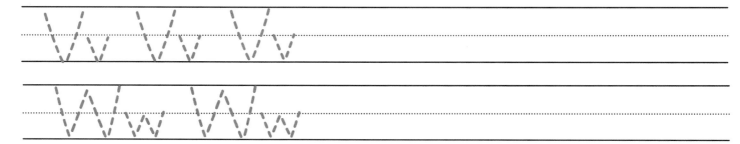

Draw a line from each picture to the correct letter.

Beginning **V**

Beginning **W**

Seeing Spots

Count the ladybugs in each group. Then add the numbers.

1.   🐞🐞🐞🐞🐞🐞🐞   +   🐞🐞🐞   =   _____

2.   🐞   +   🐞🐞🐞🐞🐞🐞🐞🐞   =   _____

3.   🐞🐞🐞   +   🐞🐞🐞   =   _____

4.   🐞🐞🐞🐞   +   🐞🐞🐞   =   _____

5.   🐞🐞🐞🐞🐞   +   🐞🐞🐞   =   _____

6.   🐞🐞🐞🐞🐞🐞🐞   +   🐞🐞🐞🐞🐞   =   _____

7.   🐞🐞   +   🐞🐞🐞🐞🐞   =   _____

8.   🐞🐞🐞🐞🐞   +   🐞🐞🐞🐞🐞   =   _____

Pattern Paths

Look at the numbers in each row. Then finish the pattern.

1.

 2 2 3 3 4

2.

2 3 4 ___ 6 ___ 8 9

3.

3 3 5 5 7 ___ 9 ___

4.

2 4 6 ___ ___ 12 14 16

5.

10 9 ___ 7 ___ 5 4 ___

Mix and Match

Follow the directions below.

mi**x**

Practice writing the letters **Xx**.

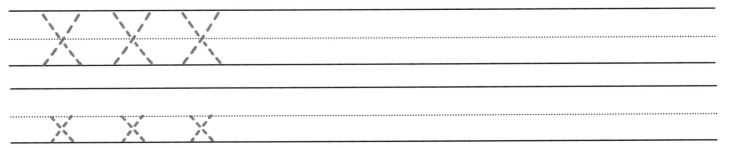

Circle the pictures that end with the **x** sound.

Draw the Word

Describing words give details about an object.
Draw an object for each word below.

Draw something furry.

Draw something tasty.

Draw something sticky.

Draw something funny.

Word Groups

Write each word in the correct circle.

bread	blue	red	square	milk
circle	grapes	star	green	pizza
triangle	brown	beans	oval	yellow

FOODS

_____

_____

_____

_____

_____

COLORS

_____

_____

_____

_____

SHAPES

_____

_____

_____

_____

Balloon Basics

Add or subtract.

1. 3
   + 6

2. 7
   − 5

3. 5
   + 0

4. 10
   − 8

5. 4
   + 3

6. 6
   − 5

7. 8
   + 1

8. 9
   − 9

9. 3
   + 7

10. 10
    + 5

11. 4
    + 4

12. 1
    − 0

Y Versus Z

Follow the directions below.

yawn

zipper

Practice writing the letters **Yy** and **Zz**.

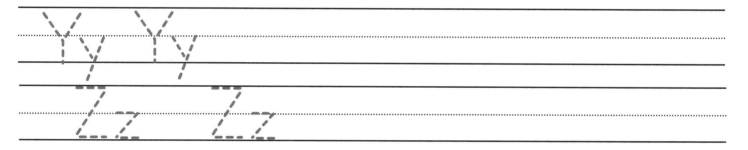

Draw a line to connect each picture with the correct letter.

Beginning **Y**

Beginning **Z**

Bears, Birds, and Bees

Circle the animal you like best. Then trace the animal names below.

bear

bee

bird

Math Match

Solve each problem. Draw a line to connect
the problems that have the same answer.

3 + 3 = 6

3 − 0 = ___

4 − 2 = ___

8 + 0 = ___

1 + 8 = ___

8 − 6 = ___

7 − 2 = ___

6 + 3 = ___

3 + 5 = ___

10 − 4 = 6

6 − 3 = ___

4 + 1 = ___

Rhyme Time

Follow the directions below.

Draw a line to match the pictures whose names rhyme.

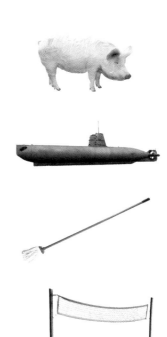

Complete the rhyming words.

m u g   __ u g   __ __ g   __ __ __ __

r a t   __ a t   __ __ t   __ __ __

Then and Now

Long ago, people used different objects to live and travel from what we use today. Use **blue** to circle the objects from long ago. Use **yellow** to circle the objects from today.

1. How do we travel?

2. How do we keep in touch with others?

3. What do we use every day?

Counting Coins

Count the coins in each row. Write the total value of each group of coins.

1¢   5¢   10¢   25¢

1. [penny] [penny] [penny]   = 3¢

2. [penny] [nickel]   = _____

3. [penny] [penny] [nickel] [nickel]   = _____

4. [dime] [dime] [dime] [dime]   = _____

5. [dime] [dime] [nickel]   = _____

6. [dime] [dime] [dime] [nickel] [penny]   = _____

7. [quarter] [nickel] [penny] [penny]   = _____

8. [quarter] [dime] [nickel] [nickel]   = _____

9. [quarter] [nickel] [nickel] [nickel] [penny] [penny]   = _____

10. [quarter] [nickel] [penny] [penny] [penny] [penny]   = _____

Count by 5s

Count by 5s and write the missing numbers.

1. **5**   **10**   **15**   **20**   ____

2. **30**   ____   **40**   ____   **50**

3. ____   **10**   ____   ____   **25**

4. ____   **35**   ____   **45**   ____

5. **25**   ____   ____   **40**   ____

6. **15**   ____   ____   ____   ____

Word Roundup

Follow the directions below.

Circle the correct word.

box	bell	fork	cat
fox	bed	fan	hat

Fill in the missing letters. Use the letters on the left to help.

m h
g l
j f
r g

__ u __　　__ ea __　　__ u __　　__ a __

Write the name of each picture. Use the words on the left to help.

dog
cab
hat
fox

_____　　_____　　_____　　_____

Circle and Subtract

Follow the directions to find the answers.

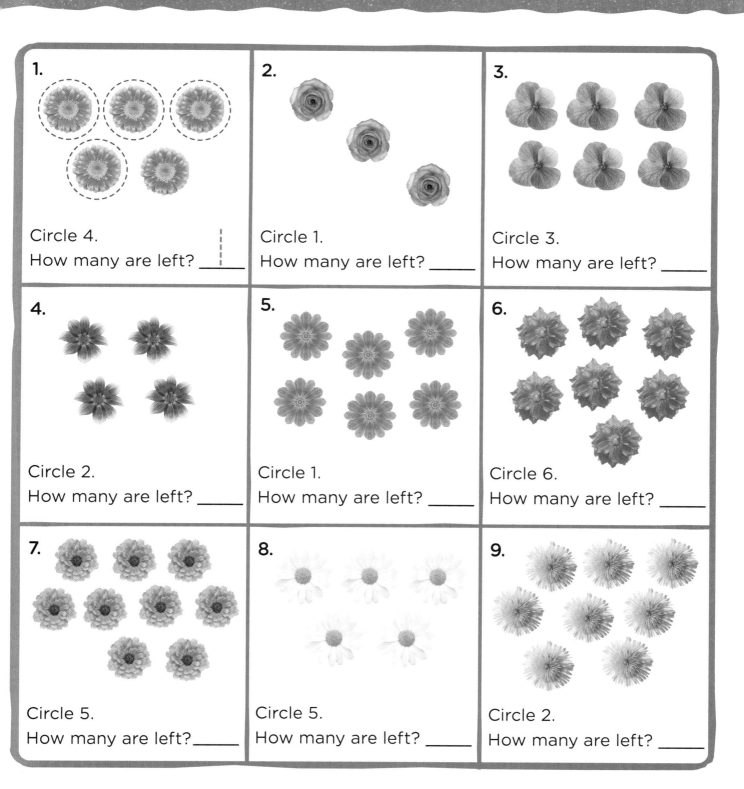

1.

Circle 4.
How many are left? _____

2.

Circle 1.
How many are left? _____

3.

Circle 3.
How many are left? _____

4.

Circle 2.
How many are left? _____

5.

Circle 1.
How many are left? _____

6.

Circle 6.
How many are left? _____

7.

Circle 5.
How many are left?_____

8.

Circle 5.
How many are left? _____

9.

Circle 2.
How many are left? _____

All Day Long

Look at each picture. Read the sentence. Circle
morning or **night** to show when you do each activity.

1. He's going to school.

(morning)   night

2. She's going to bed.

morning   night

3. She's eating breakfast.

morning   night

4. He's looking at the stars.

morning   night

5. He's eating dinner.

morning   night

6. She's getting dressed.

morning   night

It's a Date

Follow the directions below.

Number the days on the calendar 1 through 30.

JUNE

SUN	MON	TUE	WED	THU	FRI	SAT

Look at the calendar to answer the questions or follow the directions.

1. What month is the calendar for? _____

2. Circle the days of the week.

3. How many days are in a week? _____

4. Draw a star on the last day of the month.

5. How many Saturdays are in June? _____

Bonus Question:

What month is your birthday? _____

More Word Roundup

Follow the directions below.

Circle the correct word.

yarn
corn

ham
hat

jeans
queen

can
cat

Fill in the missing letters. Use the letters in the middle to help.

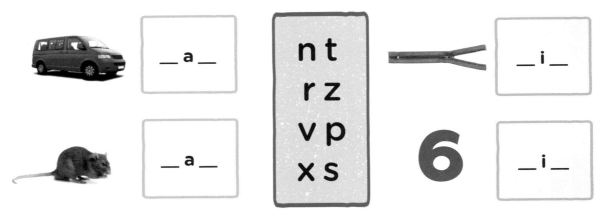

__ a __

n t
r z
v p
x s

__ i __

__ a __

6

__ i __

Write the name of each picture. Use the words on the left to help.

quiz
web
sun
vase

_____   _____   _____   _____

Build a Sandwich

Write the numbers **1** to **4** to put the steps in order.

_____

_____

_____

_____

Silly Story

Finish the story using the words in the box.

tree	peanuts	zoo	elephant
penguins	snakes	dad	toy

My family went to the ___ZOO___. We had so much fun! First,

my _____ got me a _____ lion at the gift

shop. We fed a big gray _____. We fed him lots

of _____. Then I saw a funny monkey in a_____ !

We saw more animals, too. The sign told us where to find _____

and _____. I liked the elephant best. I loved going to

the zoo!

Copy Cats

Follow the directions below.

Copy each pattern in the boxes below.

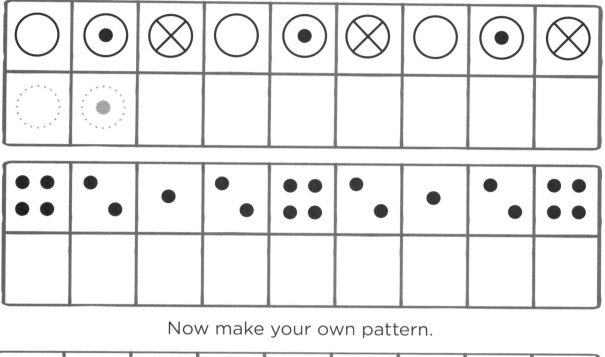

Now make your own pattern.

Copy the picture. Use the dots to help.

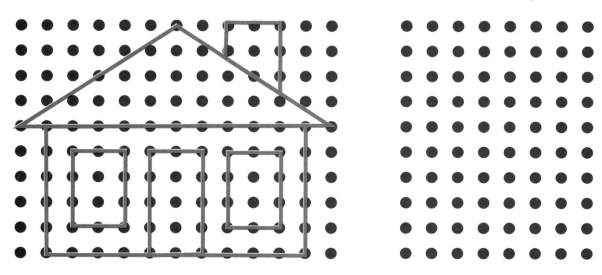

More Than One

To show there is more than one, add **s** at the end of the words.

Singular	Plural
bed	bed + s = beds

Add **s** and write the plural of each word.

1.
bell

bells

2.
key ___ ___ ___ ___

Write the singular and plural of each word.

3.
___ ___ ___

___ ___ ___

4.
___ ___ ___ ___

___ ___ ___ ___

Sometimes you add **es** to show there is more than one. Write the plurals.

5.
___ ___ ___

___ ___ ___ ___

6.
___ ___ ___

___ ___ ___ ___

Parts of a Story

With an adult, read the story. Then answer the questions.

One very hot day, Fox was walking in a field. He was very thirsty. He saw some grapes hanging from a vine. The grapes looked plump and juicy. Fox licked his dry lips. The grapes looked delicious! Fox decided he must have some grapes. He jumped high. But he could not reach the juicy fruit. Fox jumped over and over again. But the grapes were just out of reach. Finally, Fox sat down in the dirt. He was very thirsty. He was too tired to jump anymore. He said, "Those grapes are probably sour, anyway!" Fox put his nose in the air and walked away.

Say or write the answers to these questions.

1. Who is the character in this story?   _____

2. Where does the story take place?   _____

3. How does the story start?   _____

4. How does the story end?   _____

5. What was the character's problem?   _____

Peanut Butter Science

With an adult, make this fun-to-eat play dough!

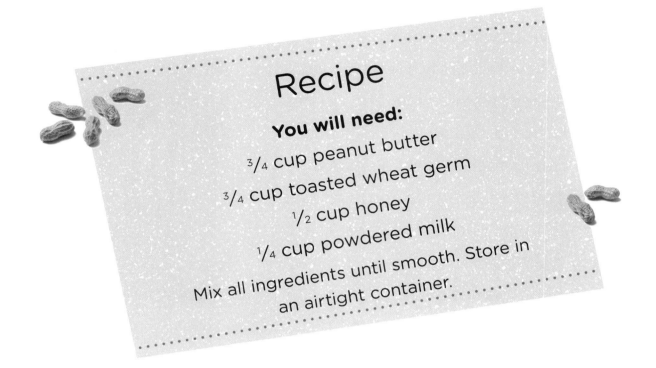

Recipe

You will need:

$3/4$ cup peanut butter

$3/4$ cup toasted wheat germ

$1/2$ cup honey

$1/4$ cup powdered milk

Mix all ingredients until smooth. Store in an airtight container.

Talk about these questions with an adult.

1. Look at each item as you put it in the bowl.
- How does it feel?
- How does it smell?
- Is it a liquid or a solid?

2. Describe the dough.
- Is it soft or hard?
- Is it wet or dry?

3. Shape the dough with your hands.
- Stretch it. Squeeze it.
- Shape it into an object.

Draw a picture of your object. You can even eat it! Yum!

I  Earth!

Learn what you can do to help Earth! Write one way you can love Earth on page **7** of your cut-out book below. Put the pages in order, then staple them together on the left side. Draw a picture.

I ♥ Earth.

1

I can water flowers.

3

I can plant trees.

5

I can _____.

7

I  Earth!

Write one way you can love Earth on
page **8** of your cut-out book below. Draw a picture, too!

I can save paper.

4

I can save water.

2

I can _____.

8

I can recycle cans and bottles.

6

Balloon Blues

If the number matches the word on each balloon, circle the balloon.
If they don't match, cross the balloon out.

Time Match

Draw a line matching the clock to the correct time.

12:30

11:00

4:30

4:00

7:30

8:00

Can You Count?

Count the objects in each row. Then draw more objects to make a total of **15**. On the line, write how many objects you added.

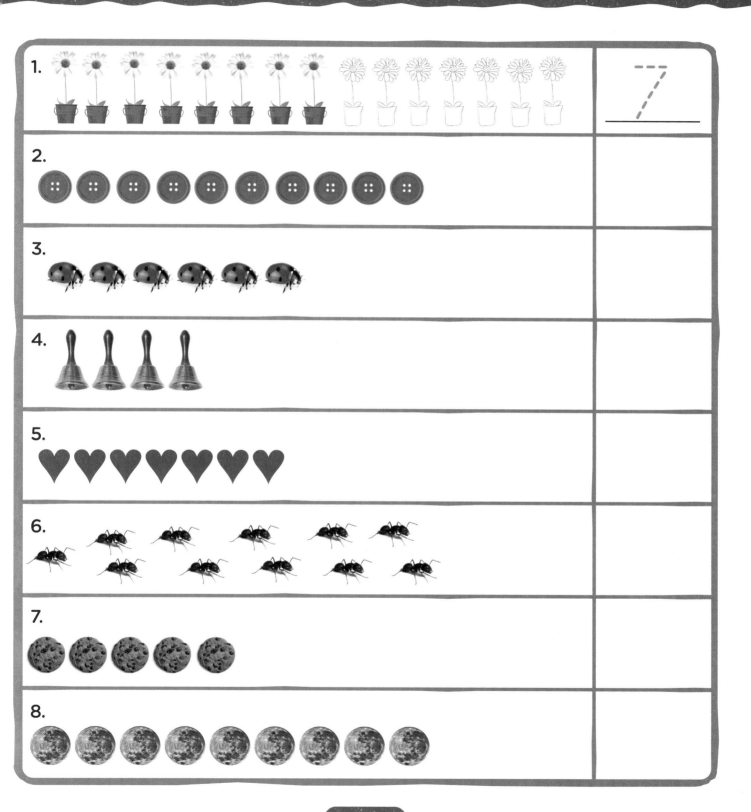

1. _7_

2.

3.

4.

5.

6.

7.

8.

The Price Is Right

Follow the directions below.

Look at the price for each item. Draw a line to the group of nickels that matches the price.

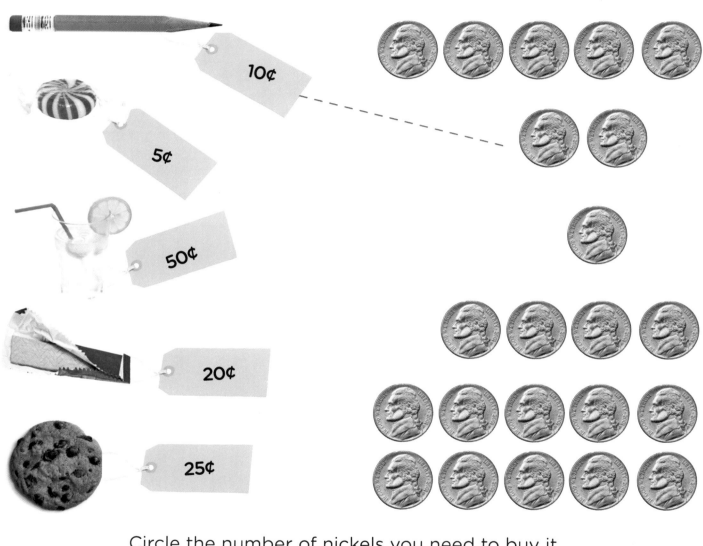

Circle the number of nickels you need to buy it.

Ready, Set, Review!

Circle the word or write the letters to name each picture.
Each time you hear a short vowel sound, that
vowel scores a point. See which vowel wins!

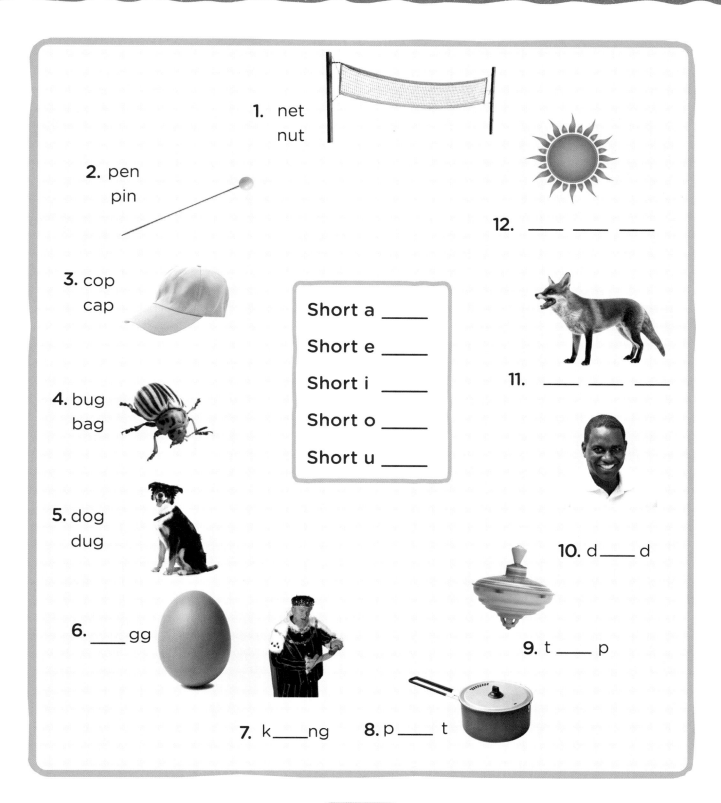

1. net
   nut

2. pen
   pin

3. cop
   cap

4. bug
   bag

5. dog
   dug

6. ___ gg

7. k ___ ng

8. p ___ t

9. t ___ p

10. d ___ d

11. ___ ___ ___

12. ___ ___ ___

Short a _____
Short e _____
Short i _____
Short o _____
Short u _____

Seeing Sounds

Say the name for each picture. Listen to the first sounds
you hear. Write the beginning sounds for each picture.
Then write the words in the crossword puzzle.

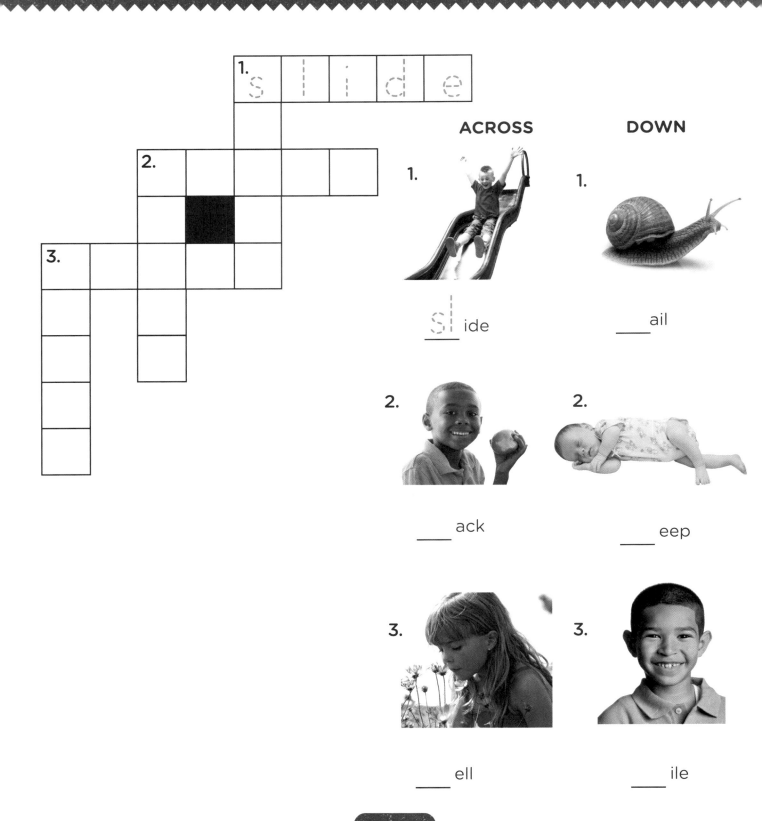

ACROSS

1.

s̲l̲ ide

2.

___ ack

3.

___ ell

DOWN

1.

___ ail

2.

___ eep

3.

___ ile

Trains on Time

Follow the directions below.

The trains were supposed to arrive at 3:00.
Connect each train with the time it arrived.

1.

One hour late

a) 2:00

2.

One hour early

b) 5:00

3.

On time

c) 3:00

4.

Two hours late

d) 4:00

Now draw the hands on each clock to show the time.

10:00

7:00

2:00

12:00

4:00

Long Vowel A

Fill in the letters that make the **long a** sound.

1.

a _ e

l___k___   v___s___   g___m___   t___p___

2.

a i

p_____l   r_____n   m_____l   m_____d

3.

a y

  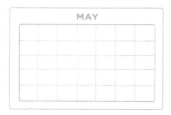 

s_____   h_____   M_____   p_____

Healthy Habits

Unscramble the word for each sentence. Write it on the line.

1. 1. Before dinner, I **S A W H** my hands.

2. I eat good **O D F O** to stay healthy and strong.

3. I **H R S B U** my teeth twice a day.

4. I wear a **E H T E M L** when I ride my bike.

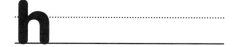

5. I drink **L I K M** for strong bones.

6. I cross the **T S T E R E** with an adult.

Where Do I Live?

Draw a line from each home to the animal or person who lives in it.

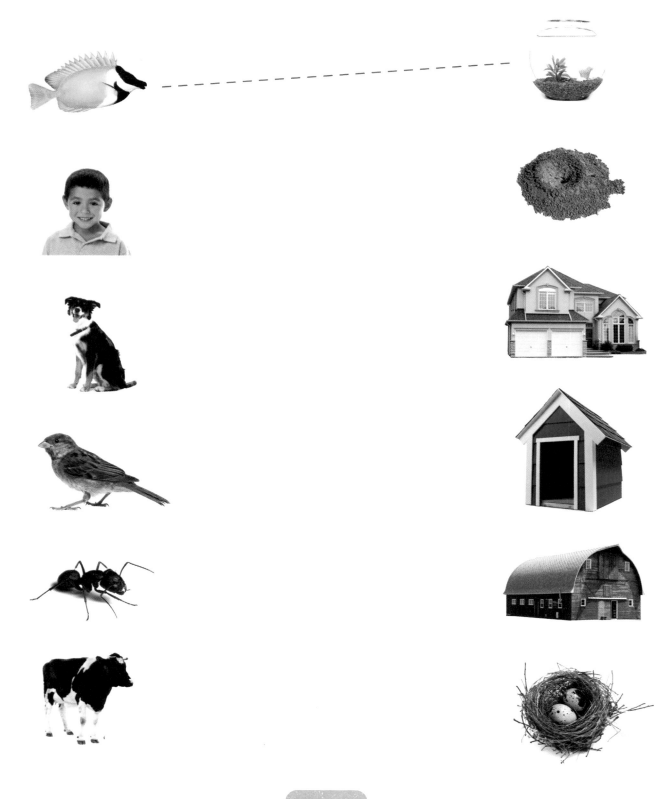

Long Vowel E

Follow the directions below.

Circle the vowel pair in each word.

1.

read   seal

jeans   ear

2.

queen   heel

see   sheep

Fill in the missing vowel pairs.

3.

l____f   t ____

l___k   b___k

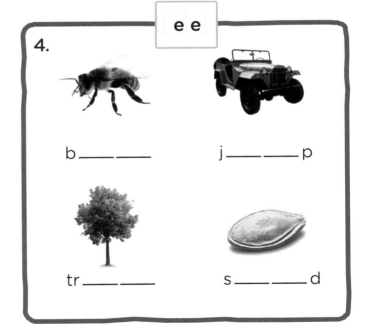

4.

b____   j____p

tr____   s___d

Pet Graph

Look at the graph. Then answer the questions.

	cat	dog	bird	fish	frog
6					
5	■				
4	■	■		■	
3	■	■	■	■	
2	■	■	■	■	
1	■	■	■	■	■

Number of People

cat   dog   bird   fish   frog

1. Which pet do people like best?

_____

2. Which pet do people like least?

_____

3. Which two pets do people like the same?

_____   _____

4. Which one of these pets do you like best? Add your answer to the graph. Does it change any of the answers above?

YES   **NO**

Terrific Teens

Follow the directions below.

Trace the numbers and count by 10s.

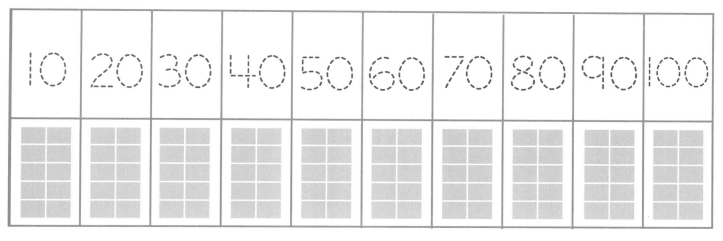

Count by tens and write the numbers.

Count the groups of ten and write the number.

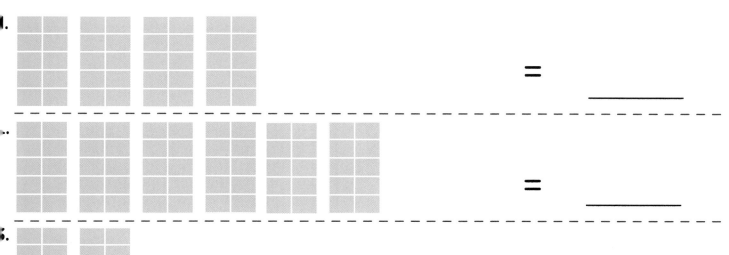

1. = _____

2. = _____

3. = _____

Long Vowel I

Fill in the letters that make the **long i** sound.

1. | i_e |

b ___ k ___   n ___ n ___   d ___ m ___   f ___ v ___

2. | i e |

t ___ ___   p ___ ___

3. | y |

fl ___   cr ___   sk ___   dr ___

Fat Cats

Write a color word from the box to finish each rhyme. The word should rhyme with the last word in the first line. Circle the cat with the matching color!

green	**pink**	**white**	**black**
blue	yellow	**brown**	**red**

1. Fuzzy is a happy fellow,

I think I will circle him _yellow_ !

2. Snowy's fur is clean and bright,

I think I will circle her _____ !

3. Sheba's tail is long and lean,

I think I will circle her _____!

4. Tiny curls up in the sink,

I think I will circle him _____!

5. Chester roams around the town,

I think I will circle him _____ !

6. Misty loves to purr and mew,

I think I will circle her _____ !

7. Tomcat sleeps upon my bed,

I think I will circle him _____!

8. Silky laps milk for a snack,

I think I will circle her_____ !

On the Farm

Unscramble the name of each farm animal. Write it on the line.

1.  W C O   COW

2.  E H N

3.  E P E H S

4.  O G D

5.  G I P

6.  U K D C

7.  T C A

8.  T A G O

Long Vowel O

Circle or fill in the letters that make the **long o** sound.

o_e

1.
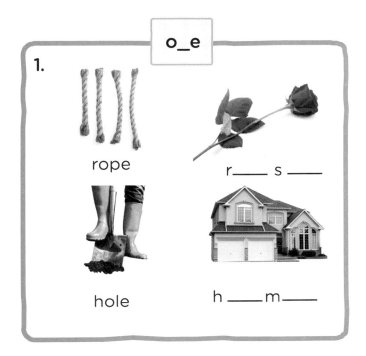

rope

r____ s____

hole

h ____ m____

o e

2.
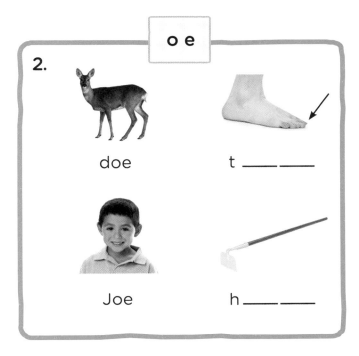

doe

t ____ ____

Joe

h ____ ____

o a

3.

loaf

b ____ ____ t

goat

c ____ ____ t

o w

4.
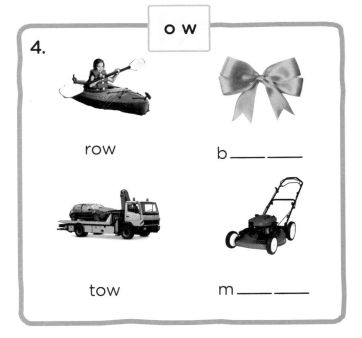

row

b ____ ____

tow

m ____ ____

Secret Message

Use the letter code below to write a secret message.
Write the letters that go with the shapes in the boxes.

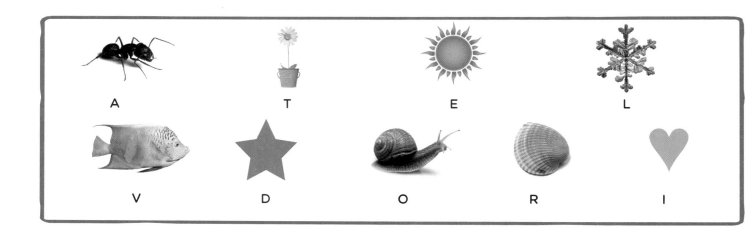

A   T   E   L

V   D   O   R   I

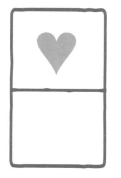

Mirror Magic

Do you know what these shapes will look like in a mirror? Find out by drawing each shape on the edge of an index card and pressing it up against a mirror. What do you see? Draw the pictures you see below.

Dime Time

Follow the directions below.

Look at the price for each item. Draw a line to the group of dimes that matches the price.

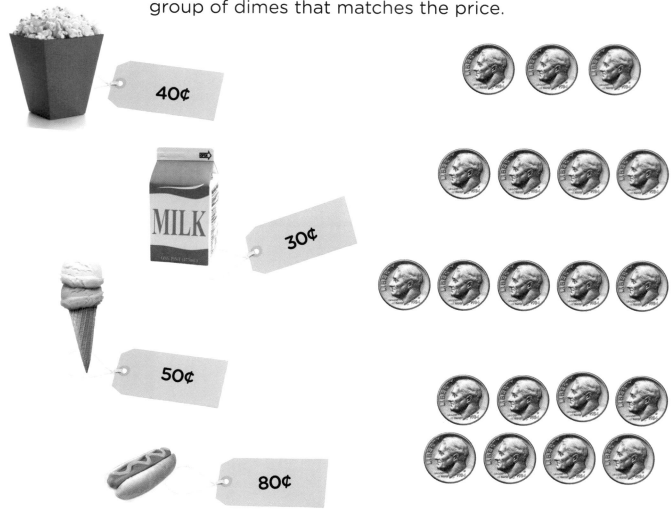

Circle the number of dimes you need to buy the juice.

Long Vowel U

Follow the directions below.

Fill in the letters that make the **long u** sound.

1.

| u _ e |

t ___ b ___   t ___ n ___   fl ___ t ___   J ___ n ___

2.

| u e |

gl ___ ___   S ___ ___   bl ___ ___   d ___ ___

Review all the vowel pairs with **silent e**. Write the name of each picture.

3.

| a _ e |
| i _ e |
| o _ e |
| u _ e |

   9

___   ___   ___   ___

Let's Travel!

Look at each picture. How does it travel? Draw a line from the picture to the word **air**, **water**, or **land**.

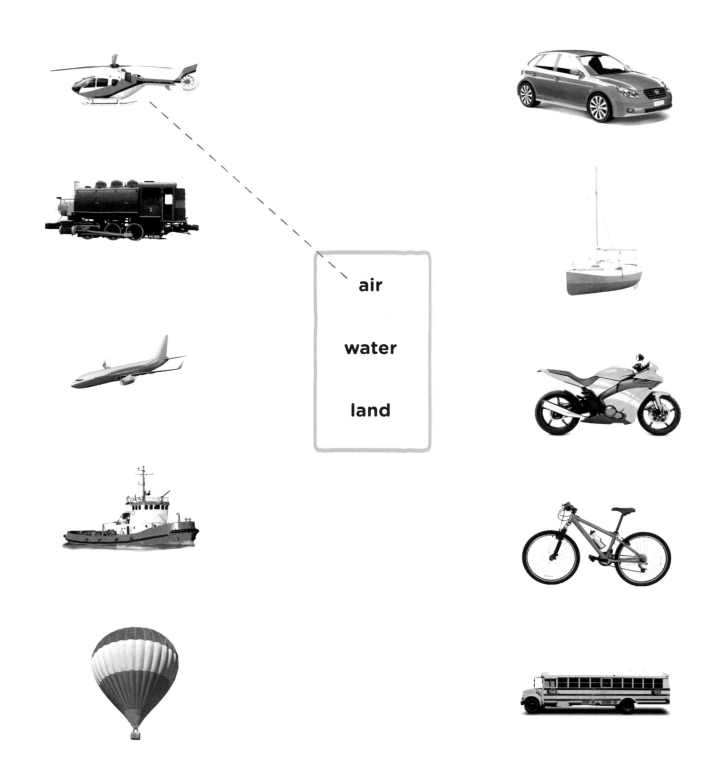

air

water

land

Two by Twos

Follow the directions below.

Count by 2s and write the missing numbers.

1.   2   ____   6   ____   10

2.   2   4   ___   ___   10   ___   14   ___   18   20

3.   Circle the train with the numbers that count by 2s.

2   4   16   8   9   10   12   16   8   20

a.

2   4   6   8   10   12   14   16   18   20

b.

Capital Competition

Follow the directions below.

Always capitalize:
The first word in the sentence
Someone's name
The word **I**

Today, **J**oe and **I** are sad.

Circle the capital letters in each group of sentences.
Count the capital letters and write it in the box.

1.
> Five kids ride the bus. Six kids ride bikes. Joe rides in a car. I like Joe. Today I ride with Joe.

2.
> I have a dog. His name is Max. I put Max in the tub. My dog Max gives me a hug. Max and I have fun.

Circle the sentences with the correct capitalization.
Cross out the incorrect sentences.

3. Joe and i ride the bus.

4. Max is a dog.

5. I ride my bike with Joe.

6. the tub is for Max.

Inching Along

Measure each object. Write the number of inches.

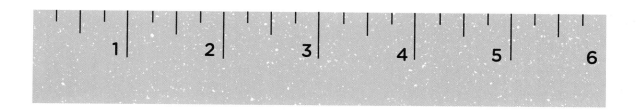

1. _____ inches

2. _____ inches

3. _____ inches

4. _____ inches

The Long Race

Circle the word that names each picture. Each time you hear a long vowel sound, that vowel scores a point. See which vowel wins!

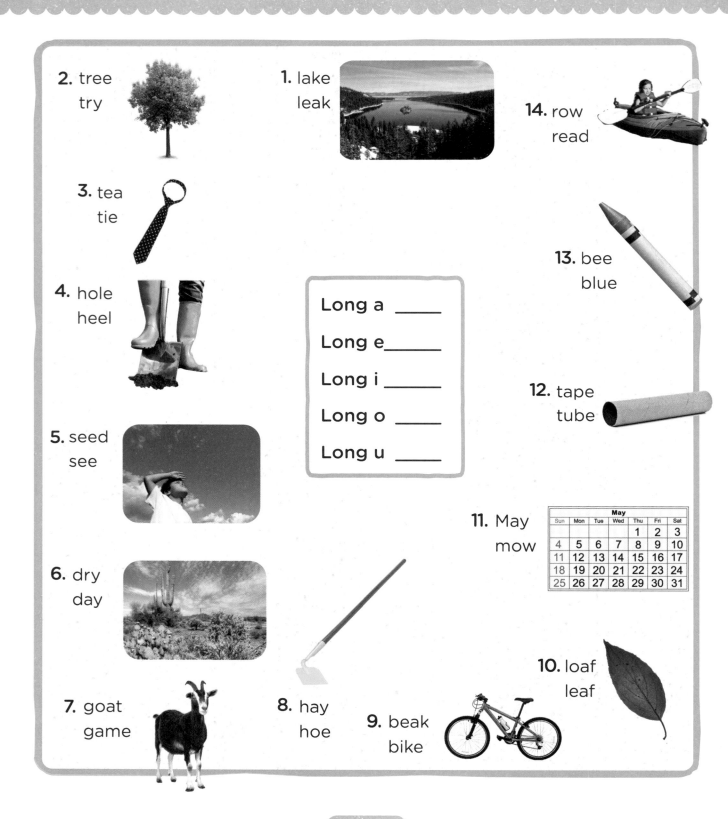

2. tree
try

3. tea
tie

4. hole
heel

5. seed
see

6. dry
day

7. goat
game

1. lake
leak

8. hay
hoe

9. beak
bike

Long a _____
Long e_____
Long i _____
Long o _____
Long u _____

11. May
mow

10. loaf
leaf

14. row
read

13. bee
blue

12. tape
tube

Garden Graph

Follow the directions below.

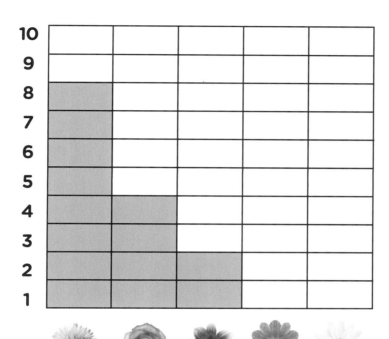

Read the sentences and complete the graph.

There are 6 in the garden.

There are 3 in the garden.

Use the graph to solve the problems.

1. How many ? _____

2. How many  ? _____

3. = _____

4. = _____

5. + = _____

6. = _____

Silly Sentences

Draw a line from each sentence to its matching picture.

1. A fly is on the pie.

a)

2. The queen is in jeans.

b)

3. The glue is blue.

c)

d)

4. The mail is in the pail.

e)

5. The goat is on a boat.

Greater or Less?

Follow the directions below.

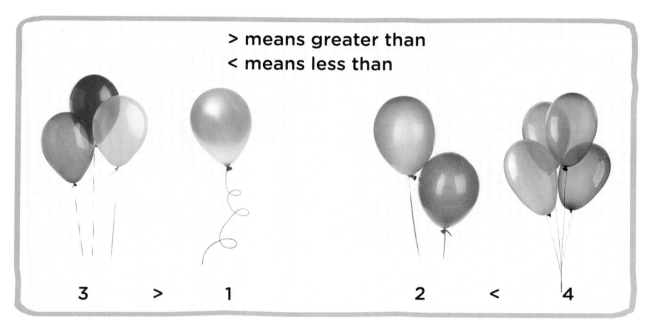

> means greater than
< means less than

3 > 1

2 < 4

Fill in > or <.

1. 3 _____ 10

2. 8 _____ 4

3. 15 _____ 5

4. 3 _____ 13

5. 20 _____ 2

6. 32 _____ 23

7. 40 _____ 50

8. 16 _____ 61

9. 7 _____ 77

10. 80 _____ 58

11. 69 _____ 99

12. 100 _____ 10

Long and Short Sort

Draw a line from each picture to the short or long vowels box.

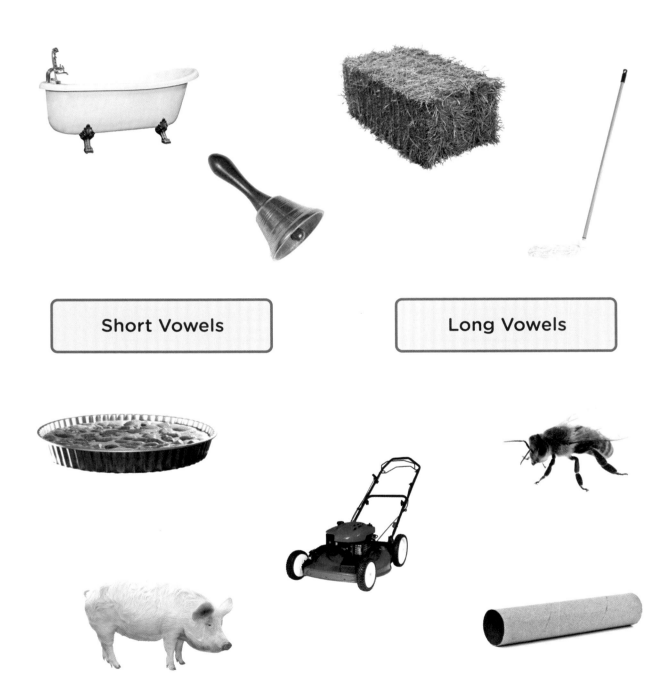

| Short Vowels | Long Vowels |

Coin Count

Match the group of coins that equal the same amount.

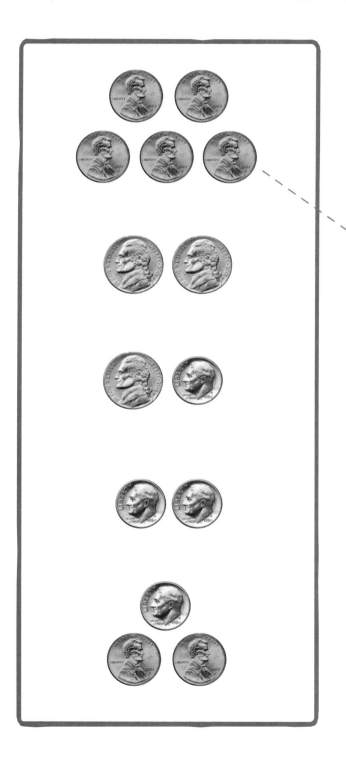

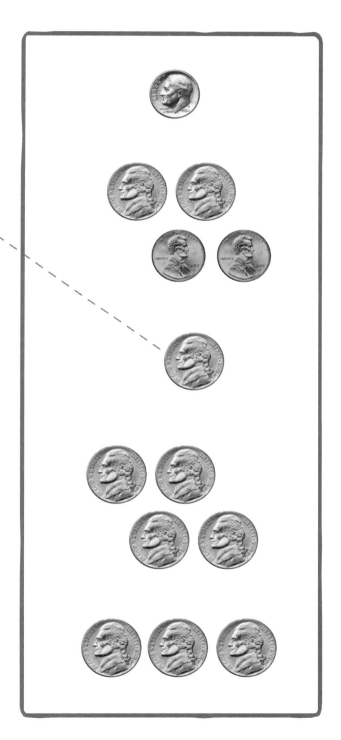

End Game

Follow the directions below.

Use a **.** to end a statement.   **You are Joe.**

Use a **?** to end a question.   **Are you Joe?**

Use a **!** to add emphasis.   **You are not Joe!**

Circle the punctuation at the end of each sentence.
Count how many of each kind. See which mark has the highest number.

Max has a box. What is in the box? Is it a sock? No, it's not a sock. Is it a cap? No, it's not a cap. Open the box, Max! What do you see? It's a pie!

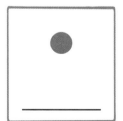      

Read each sentence. Add a period or a question mark.

1. Why are you sad   **2.** You are in the tub

3. The bug is on the rug   **4.** Are you in the car

Cool Clocks

Follow the directions below.

3:00

3:30

To show time to the half hour, the big hand is on the 6. The little hand is always halfway between the two numbers.

Circle the correct time.

1.

3:00
3:30

2.

8:00
8:30

3.

10:00
10:30

Draw the hands on each clock.

4.

2:30

5.

7:30

6.

4:30

Answer Key

Page 4

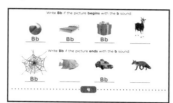

Page 5

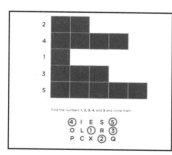

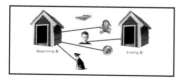

Page 6

The following pictures are circled:
cup, crab, and cat.

Page 7

2. 4 + 1 = 5
3. 3 + 2 = 5
4. 2 + 2 = 4
5. 3 + 4 = 7
6. 1 + 5 = 6
7. 1 + 3 = 4
8. 4 + 4 = 8

Page 8

2. 12 or 9 (circled)
3. 7 or 6 (circled)
4. 9 or 8 (circled)
5. 5 (circled) or 7
6. 10 or 9 (circled)

Page 9

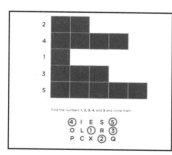

Page 10

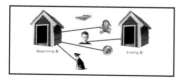

Page 11

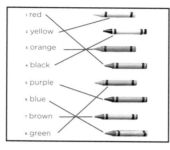

Page 12

2. c
3. b
4. w
5. s
6. h
7. l
8. p
9. g
10. k
11. r
12. d

Page 13

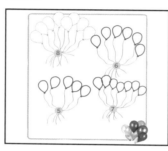

Page 14

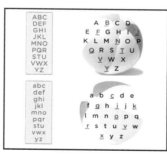

Page 15

Answers will vary.

Page 16

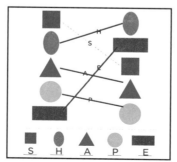

Page 17

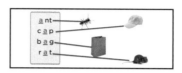

Page 18

2. tennis racket
3. book
4. car
5. fox
6. hippo

Page 19

2. 11:30
3. 5:30
4. 9:00
5. 12:00
6. 8:30

Page 20

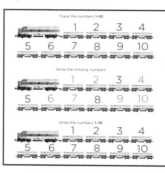

Page 21

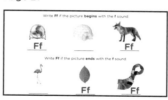

Page 22

2. bear
3. cat
4. deer
5. fox
6. hippo
7. lion
8. mouse
9. owl
10. pig
11. snake
12. whale

Page 23

Page 24

2. pail
3. dog
4. stop
5. fan
6. bat
7. bed
8. lock

Page 25

2. leaf
3. stem
4. roots

Page 26

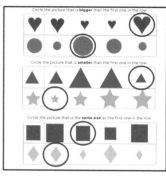

Page 27

The following pictures are circled:
hand, hat, horse.

Page 28

Page 29

2. square
3. triangle
4. triangle
5. circle
6. square
7. circle
8. square
9. triangle

Page 30

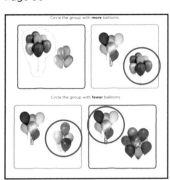

Page 31

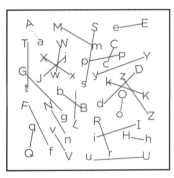

Page 32

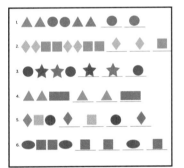

Page 33

2. 4	10. 6
3. 5	11. 8
4. 7	12. 8
5. 5	13. 7
6. 2	14. 10
7. 2	15. 1
8. 6	16. 9
9. 6	

Page 34

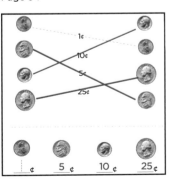

Page 35

Page 36

These objects should be circled: grapes, ape, plane, snake, sail, gate.

Page 37

These objects should be circled: seal, bee, sheep, deer, tree, leaf.

Page 38

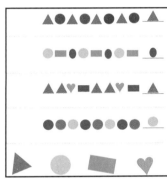

Page 39

The following pictures are circled: jet, jeep, jeans.

Page 40

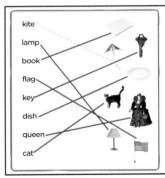

Page 41

2. forest
3. rain forest
4. ocean

Page 42

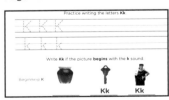

Page 43

This page is complete when the words are traced. Answers to the question will vary.

Page 44

2. 2 quarters
3. 3 dimes, 2 nickels
4. 2 dimes, 1 nickel, 2 pennies; or 3 nickels, 1 dime, 2 pennies
5. 1 quarter, 2 nickels, 3 pennies
6. 2 quarters, 1 dime, 1 penny

Page 45

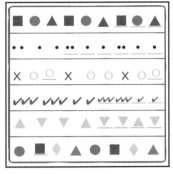

Page 46

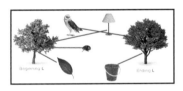

Page 47

2. horse
3. chair
4. piggybank
5. crayon
6. daisy
7. bicycle
8. bee

Page 48

2. $2\frac{1}{2}$ inches
3. 1 inch
4. 3 inches
5. $2\frac{1}{2}$ inches

Page 49

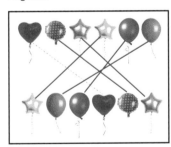

Page 50

Words with 2 letters: in, an, it, at
Words with 3 letters: tan, ran, rat, tar, art, ant
Word with 4 letters: rain
The BIG word: train

Page 51

Page 52

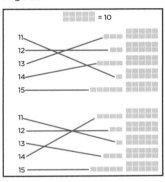

Page 53

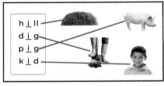

Page 54

The following words are circled: eye, bike, dime, ice, mice, five.

Page 55

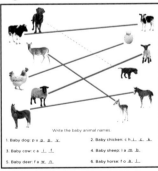

Page 56

2. 5
3. 4
4. 3
5. 6

Page 57

Page 58
2. less 4. more
3. more 5. less
6. less

Page 59

Page 60
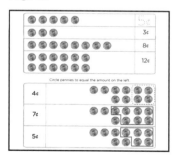

Page 61
This page is complete when the words are traced and a picture is drawn at the bottom. Answers to the question will vary.

Page 62
2. 7 4. 5
3. 8 5. 6

Page 63
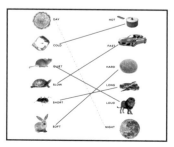

Page 64
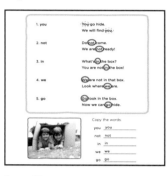

Page 65
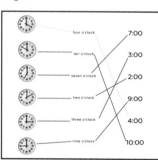

Page 66
2. read 5. goat
3. boat 6. leaf
4. seal 7. soap
8. meat

Page 67
2. $9 - 1 = 8$ 5. $2 - 2 = 0$
3. $4 - 1 = 3$ 6. $3 - 3 = 0$
4. $6 - 1 = 5$

Page 68
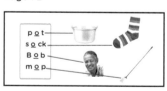

Page 69
These objects should be circled: soap, rope, hoe, toe, bow.

Page 70
2. fall 6. fall
3. summer 7. spring
4. spring 8. winter
5. winter 9. fall
10. summer

Page 71

Page 72
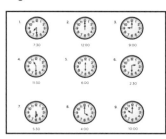

Page 73
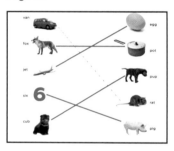

Page 74
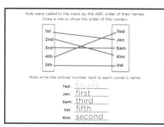

Page 75
1. $4 + 2 = 6$
2. $3 + 2 = 5$
3. $5 + 3 = 8$
4. $2 + 5 = 7$
5. $3 + 3 = 6$

Page 76
These objects should be circled: quiz, quarter, question mark, queen.

Page 77
These objects should be circled: unicorn, spoon, broom, cube, flute, glue.

Page 78
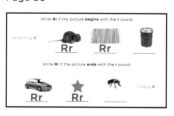

Page 79
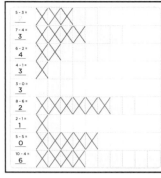

Page 80
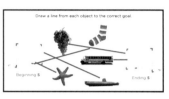

Page 81
2. lake, steak 5. ring, swing
3. bee, sea 6. rain, plane
4. sock, rock

Page 82
2. smell 6. smell
3. hear 7. feel
4. see 8. see
5. taste 9. hear

Page 83
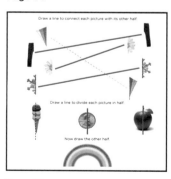

Page 84
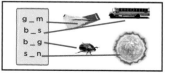

Page 85
2. read 5. teeth
3. fires 6. safe
4. pet

Page 86
2. 1 6. 2
3. 5 7. 2
4. 0 8. 1
5. 1 9. 5

Page 87
2. $2 + 2 = 4$ 5. $8 - 3 = 5$
3. $5 + 4 = 9$ 6. $10 - 3 = 7$

Page 88
1. football
2. doghouse
3. mailbox
4. anthill

Page 89
2. e 6. o
3. u 7. a
4. e 8. u
5. i 9. o

Page 90

Page 91

Page 92

2. S
3. Q
4. S
5. Q
6. Q
7. S
8. S
9. Q
10. S

Page 93

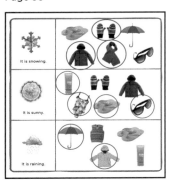

Page 94

Page 95

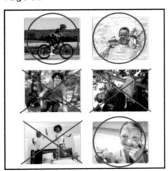

Page 96

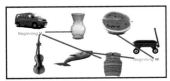

Page 97

2. 1 + 7 = 8
3. 3 + 3 = 6
4. 4 + 3 = 7
5. 5 + 3 = 8
6. 7 + 5 = 12
7. 2 + 5 = 7
8. 5 + 5 = 10

Page 98

2. 2 3 4 5 6 7 8 9
3. 3 3 5 5 7 7 9 9
4. 2 4 6 8 10 12 14 16
5. 10 9 8 7 6 5 4 3

Page 99

The following pictures should be circled: fox, 6, axe, box.

Page 100

Answers will vary.

Page 101

Foods: bread, grapes, beans, milk, pizza. Colors: blue, brown, red, green, yellow. Shapes: circle, triangle, star, square, oval.

Page 102

1. 9
2. 2
3. 5
4. 2
5. 7
6. 1
7. 9
8. 0
9. 10
10. 15
11. 8
12. 1

Page 103

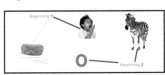

Page 104

This page is complete when an animal is circled and the words are traced.

Page 105

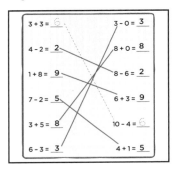

Page 106

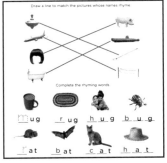

Page 107

Page 108

2. 6¢
3. 12¢
4. 40¢
5. 25¢
6. 36¢
7. 32¢
8. 45¢
9. 42¢
10. 34¢

Page 109

These missing numbers should be filled in:
1. 15; 25
2. 35; 45
3. 5; 15; 20
4. 30; 40; 50
5. 30; 35; 45
6. 20; 25; 30; 35

Page 110

Page 111

2. 2
3. 3
4. 2
5. 5
6. 1
7. 4
8. 0
9. 6

Page 112

2. night
3. morning
4. night
5. night
6. morning

Page 113

1. June
2. This question is answered when the days of the week are circled on the calendar.
3. 7
4. This question is answered when there is a star drawn on June 30.
5. 4
Bonus Question: Answers will vary.

Page 114

Page 115

Page 116

My family went to the **zoo**. We had so much fun! First, my **dad** got me a **toy** lion at the gift shop. We fed a big gray **elephant**. We fed him lots of **peanuts**. Then I saw a funny monkey in a **tree**! We saw more animals too. The sign told us where to find **penguins** and **snakes**. I liked the elephant the best. I loved going to the zoo!

Page 117

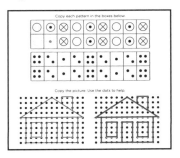

Page 118

2. keys
3. car; cars
4. doll; dolls
5. box; boxes
6. bus; buses

Page 119

1. Fox
2. a field
3. Fox was walking in the field.
4. Fox walked away from the grapes.
5. He was thirsty, and he couldn't reach the grapes.

Page 120

Answers will vary.

Pages 121 and 122

Pictures and ideas for helping Earth will vary.

Page 123

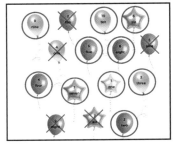

Page 124

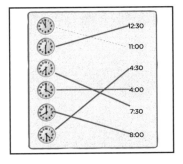

Page 125

2. 5	6. 4
3. 9	7. 10
4. 11	8. 6
5. 8	

Page 126

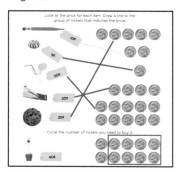

Page 127

1. net	5. dog	9. top
2. pin	6. egg	10. dad
3. cap	7. king	11. fox
4. bug	8. pot	12. sun

Short a: 2 tally marks
Short e: 2 tally marks
Short i: 2 tally marks
Short o: 4 tally marks
Short u: 2 tally marks

Page 128

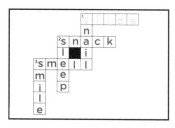

Page 129

1. d	3. c
2. a	4. b

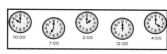

Page 130

1. lake; vase; game; tape
2. pail; rain; mail; maid
3. say; hay; May; pay

Page 131

2. food	4. helmet
3. brush	5. milk
	6. street

Page 132

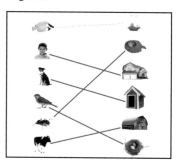

Page 133

Page 134

1. cat   3. dog; fish
2. frog   4. Answers will vary.

Page 135

10; 20; 30; 40; 50; 60; 70; 80; 90; 100
1. 40
2. 60
3. 20

Page 136

1. bike; nine; dime; five
2. tie; pie
3. fly; cry; sky; dry

Page 137

2. white	5. brown
3. green	6. blue
4. pink	7. red
	8. black

Page 138

2. hen	6. duck
3. sheep	7. cat
4. dog	8. goat
5. pig	

Page 139

Page 140

I love to read!

Page 141

Page 142

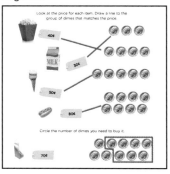

Page 143

1. tube; tune; flute; June
2. glue; Sue; blue; due
3. lake; nine; rose; tube

Page 144

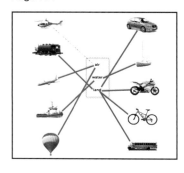

Page 145

These missing numbers should be filled in:
1. 4; 8
2. 6; 8; 12; 16
3. b

Page 146

1. 8
2. 9
3. Joe and i ride the bus. [Cross out sentence.]
4. Max is a dog. [Circle sentence.]
5. I ride my bike with Joe. [Circle sentence.]
6. the tub is for Max. [Cross out sentence.]

Page 147

1. 2	3. 1
2. 4	4. 6

Page 148

1. lake	6. dry	11. May
2. tree	7. goat	12. tube
3. tie	8. hoe	13. blue
4. hole	9. bike	14. row
5. see	10. leaf	

Long a: 2 tally marks
Long e: 3 tally marks
Long i: 3 tally marks
Long o: 4 tally marks
Long u: 2 tally marks

Page 149

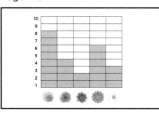

1. 4	3. 10	5. 10
2. 8	4. 11	6. 4

Page 150

1. b	3. a	5. e
2. d	4. c	

Page 151

1. ‹	5. ›	9. ‹
2. ›	6. ›	10. ›
3. ›	7. ‹	11. ‹
4. ‹	8. ‹	12. ›

Page 152

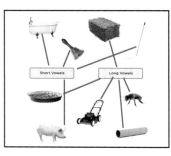

Page 153

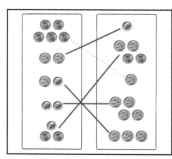

Page 154

Missing answers: 3 periods, 4 question marks, 2 exclamation points
1. Why are you sad**?**
2. You are in the tub**.**
3. The bug is on the rug**.**
4. Are you in the car**?**

Page 155

1. 3:00
2. 8:00
3. 10:30

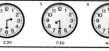

WEEK 1
COMPLETE!

PERFECT! PERFECT! PERFECT! PERFECT!

WEEK 2
COMPLETE!

WEEK 3
COMPLETE!

PERFECT! PERFECT! PERFECT! PERFECT!

WEEK 4
COMPLETE!

WOW! WOW! WOW! WOW!

WEEK 5
COMPLETE!

WOW! WOW! WOW! WOW!

WEEK 6
COMPLETE!

SUPER! SUPER! SUPER! SUPER!

WEEK 7
COMPLETE!

SUPER! SUPER! SUPER! SUPER!

FANTASTIC! FANTASTIC! FANTASTIC! FANTASTIC!

WEEK 8
COMPLETE!

WELL DONE! WELL DONE! WELL DONE! WELL DONE!

WEEK 9
COMPLETE!

WEEK 10
COMPLETE!

Excellent Work! Excellent Work! Excellent Work! Excellent Work!

YOU'RE A STAR! YOU'RE A STAR! YOU'RE A STAR! YOU'RE A STAR! YOU'RE A STAR!

Excellent Work!	Excellent Work!	Excellent Work!	Excellent Work!	Excellent Work!
Excellent Work!	Excellent Work!	Excellent Work!	Excellent Work!	Excellent Work!
GREAT JOB!	GREAT JOB!	GREAT JOB!	GREAT JOB!	GREAT JOB!
GREAT JOB!	GREAT JOB!	GREAT JOB!	GREAT JOB!	GREAT JOB!
Hard Worker!	Hard Worker!	Hard Worker!	Hard Worker!	Hard Worker!
Hard Worker!	Hard Worker!	Hard Worker!	Hard Worker!	Hard Worker!
TERRIFIC WORK!	TERRIFIC WORK!	TERRIFIC WORK!	TERRIFIC WORK!	TERRIFIC WORK!
TERRIFIC WORK!	TERRIFIC WORK!	TERRIFIC WORK!	TERRIFIC WORK!	TERRIFIC WORK!
YOU'RE A STAR!	YOU'RE A STAR!	YOU'RE A STAR!	YOU'RE A STAR!	YOU'RE A STAR!

FlashKids

Punch out flash cards!

Carl is tired and hungry from a long trip. Which of these things does he need?

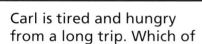

Which picture ends with the **b** sound?

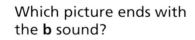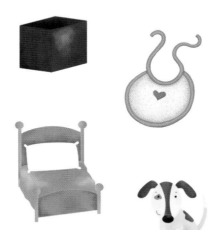

Say the name of each picture aloud. What is the letter of the first sound in each word?

1.

   d   c   b

2.

   h   j   l

3.

   p   g   n

1

3

5

Can you think of three-letter words that start with the **c** sound?

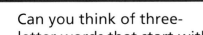

Mary loves animals. Say the name of each animal. Which animals can she keep as pets?

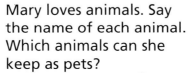

A compound word is made up of two words. Which pair does **not** form a compound word?

a.

   sun   +   rise   =

b.

   ant   +   hill   =

c.

   cat   +   dog   =

7

9

11

The mice have escaped! How many gray mice are there? Count them.

Which shape has 3 sides?

Callie lost her ants. How many ants can you find? Count them.

6   **4**   **2**

Summer camp starts at 8 AM. Which clock shows what time camp starts?

a.  _____ **:** _____

b.  _____ **:** _____

c.  _____ **:** _____

Nate blew up 4 balloons. Manny blew up 7 balloons. Write a number sentence that shows how many balloons Nate and Manny blew up together.

_____ + _____ = _____

Complete the math sentences.

a. _____ + 3 = 4

b. 2 + _____ = 7

c. 5 + _____ = 10

d. 6 + _____ = 8

12   **10**   **8**

Punch out flash cards!

Say the name of each picture aloud. Which ends with a **d** sound?

13

Amanda is going to the beach. Which items should she take?

15

Tim likes to play Scrabble. Try to make up as many words as you can using the letters he has. (Hint: You can't use letters twice.)

T U L S R E N

17

Franny loves anything with the letter F in it. Her fish is named Daffy. Her favorite food is French toast. Even her favorite state is Florida. Which item do you think she would like?

19

Correct the capitalization in each sentence.

1. clarissa and i saw a movie.

2. the Movie was called shrek.

3. we Liked it a lot.

4. We can't Wait to see part 2.

21

Britney went to the store to buy some candy. She bought 2 lollipops for 15¢ each and 2 chocolate bars for 50¢ each. How much money did she spend?

a. $1.15

b. $1.30

c. $1.70

23

FlashKids

Punch out flash cards!

Kayla collected seashells at the beach. How many of each kind did she collect? Count them. Which did she collect the most of?

Kareem wants to buy an ice cream cone with sprinkles. The cone costs $1.00 and the sprinkles are an extra 35¢. Count how much money he has. Does he have enough?

I am a number between 1 and 5. If you add me to 6, I am equal to 9. What number am I?

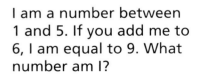

18

16

14

Unscramble each group of letters to make a word.

1. rflewo

2. lains

3. hsrbu

4. gfor

5. rete

Solve the riddles.

1. I have a face but no eyes. I have hands that move. I can be very loud. What am I?

2. I can fly very fast and far without food or rest. My wings are strong. What am I?

What do all these math problems have in common?

$3 + 4 =$

$2 + 5 =$

$1 + 6 =$

$7 + 0 =$

24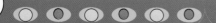

22

20

Count the coins. What is the amount?

1.

$_____

2.

$_____

25

Carly bought a box of 24 pencils. She gave 6 to her little sister. Write a number sentence.

24 – _____ = _____

Then Carly gave 7 pencils to her little brother. Write a number sentence.

_____ – 7 = _____

How many pencils did she have left?

27

Lisa is 7 years old. She is 6 years older than her little brother Michael, but 3 years younger than her older brother Mark. How much older is Mark than Michael? (Hint: Write number sentences to figure out the answer.)

29

Deirdre loves to read. Last year she read 14 books. She wants to read more than that this year. So far she has read 4. How many more does she have to read to beat last year's total?

31

An orange costs 25¢. How many different coin combinations can you think of that make up 25¢?

33

Name each shape.

1.   2.   3.

4.   5.

6.   7.

35

Count the vowels in each sentence.

1. Maggie's favorite food is pizza.
2. Jeremy likes to play soccer and baseball.
3. Cats and dogs can be friends.

30

Randy wrote a letter to his friend. Which words should be capitalized?

dear Johnny,

We are having so much fun here in florida. Yesterday we went to disney world. I was so excited to meet mickey mouse.

Talk to you soon,

Randy

28

Find these words in the word puzzle.

fan nest fox ant mop

n	e	s	t	n
j	f	o	x	m
f	a	z	a	o
q	n	y	n	p
c	n	u	t	g

26

The word **cat** and **bat** rhyme. Can you think of other words that rhyme with these two?

36

Count the vowels in this paragraph. How many are there of each?

Jenny and her family are going on vacation. They are going to be on a plane for 5 hours. Jenny says, "I will bring my music player and a book so I don't get bored."

A   E   I
___   ___   ___

O   U
___   ___

34

Find these words in the word puzzle.

sun   fun   beach
sand   swim   wave

f	r	k	l	p	o	p
m	j	u	n	s	u	n
q	t	c	n	a	u	f
s	w	a	e	n	g	u
w	a	v	e	d	h	n
i	d	s	y	k	v	x
m	e	b	e	a	c	h

32

Sammy has 14 nickels. Help him count by 5's to figure out how much money he has.

5, 10, _____, 20, _____, _____, 35, _____, _____, _____, _____, _____, _____, _____

How much money does he have?

37

Count the dots on the top of the frog's head. How many do you see?

39

Which number sentences add up to 21?

a. 4 + 17 =

b. 11 + 11 =

c. 9 + 7 =

d. 15 + 6 =

e. 9 + 12 =

f. 10 + 11 =

41

Add the numbers. Solve the riddle using the letters.

a. 5 + 3   = _____ = U
b. 6 + 5   = _____ = N
c. 9 + 4   = _____ = T
d. 17 + 6 = _____ = F
e. 15 + 4 = _____ = H
f. 13 + 8 = _____ = S
g. 12 + 14 = _____ = I
h. 14 + 8 = _____ = E

___ ___ ___
23 8   11

___ ___   ___ ___ ___
26 11   13 19 22

___ ___ ___
21 8   11

43

Dear Caregiver,

The summer months provide plenty of time to prepare your learner for the new school year. During this time, it is important not only to review the skills your student is familiar with, but also to introduce new skills your student will be learning in the coming grade. Encourage your learner to work on the cards independently or review them together so you can provide help and encouragement when needed. The cards can be used as:

- An extra practice lesson
- A take-along activity
- Daily reinforcement
- Comprehensive review

This deck contains 44 questions reviewing math and language arts skills. An answer key is provided on cards 46–48.

Enjoy!

45

Card 21
1. Clarrisa, I
2. The, movie, Shrek
3. We, liked
4. wait

Card 22
1. a clock   2. plane

Card 23
b

Card 24
1. flower 2. snail 3. brush
4. frog 5. tree

Card 25
1. 66¢   2. 92¢

Card 26

n	e	s	t	n
j	f	o	x	m
f	a	z	a	o
q	n	y	n	p
c	n	u	t	g

Card 27
24-6=18
18-7=11
Answer: She had 11 pencils left.

Card 28
Capitalized: Dear, Florida, Disney World, Mickey Mouse

Card 29
Lisa = 7
Michael = 7-6 = 1
Mark = 7+3 = 10
Mark-Michael = 10-1
Answer: Mark is 9 years older than Michael.

Card 30
1. 12 2. 12 3. 7

Card 31
More than 10

Card 32

f	r	k	l	p	o	p
m	j	u	n	s	u	n
q	t	c	n	a	u	f
s	w	a	e	n	g	u
w	a	v	e	d	h	n
i	d	s	y	k	v	x
m	e	b	e	a	c	h

Card 33
Possible answers include:
5 nickels
4 dimes, 1 nickel
4 dimes, 5 pennies

47

FlashKids

Punch out flash cards!

A noun is a person, place, or thing. A verb is an action word. Tell whether each word is a noun or a verb.

1. horse

2. take

3. house

4. car

5. run

6. sit

42

Fill in the blanks to tell what the boy is eating.

1. ch__cke__

2. __ota__es

3. p__ __s

40

Say the name of each picture. Which has a beginning **g** sound?

38

Card 34
44 vowels
a = 11; e = 11; i = 9;
o = 13 u = 2

Card 35
1. square   2. triangle
3. circle   4. diamond
5. rectangle 6. heart
7. oval

Card 36
Possible answers: at, rat, sat, mat, brat, chat, fat, hat, that

Card 37
5, 10, 15, 20, 25, 30, 35, 40, 45, 50, 55, 60, 65, 70
He has 70¢.

Card 38
gum

Card 39
5

Card 40
1. chicken   2. potatoes
3. peas

Card 41
a, d, e, f

Card 42
1. noun 2. verb 3. noun
4. noun 5. verb 6. verb

Card 43
a. 8   b. 11 c. 13 d. 23
e. 19 f. 21 g. 26 h. 22
Fun in the sun

Card 44
possible answers:
1. yummy, tasty
2. hate, dislike
3. chilly, cold
4. giant, big

Card 1
bed, food

Card 2
11

Card 3
bib

Card 4
triangle

Card 5
1. b   2. l   3. p

Card 6
4

Card 7
Possible answers: cat, can, car, cap, cab

Card 8
a. 1   b. 5   c. 5   d. 2

Card 9
cat, dog, snake, mouse, pig

Card 10
4+7=11

Card 11
c

Card 12
b

Card 13
bed

Card 14
3

Card 15
sunglasses, sunscreen

Card 16
$1.50; Kareem has enough money.

Card 17
Possible answers: rent, run, sun, true, nest, nurse, rest, rust, nut, let, lets

Card 18
6 yellow seashells, 8 blue seashells, 7 pink seashells. She collected more blue seashells.

Card 19
leaf

Card 20
All equal to 7.

Think of a word to replace the underlined word or words in each sentence.

1. My mom's spaghetti and meatballs is <u>delicious</u>.

2. I <u>don't like</u> it when my brother picks on me.

3. The ocean water was <u>freezing</u>.

4. I made a <u>huge</u> sand castle.

48   **46**   **44**

1st Grade

Track your progress throughout the summer!

Add a sticker after completing each set of activity pages. Do one set a week!

When all 10 weeks are finished you have earned your certificate!

Progress Chart

Summer Week	Activities	Date Completed	Award Sticker
1	Pages 4–18		
2	Pages 19–34		
3	Pages 35–50		
4	Pages 51–66		
5	Pages 67–82		
6	Pages 83–98		
7	Pages 99–114		
8	Pages 115–130		
9	Pages 131–146		
10	Pages 147–155		

CONGRATULATIONS!

Presented to:

_____

for successfully completing all ten sections of the

FLASH KIDS 1ST GRADE SUMMER WORKBOOK

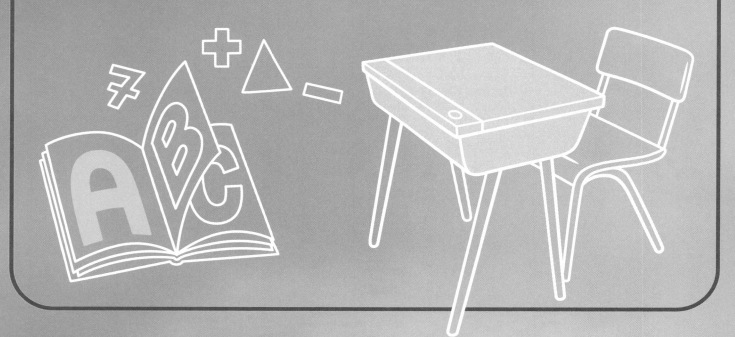